STUDENT CAPITAL™

Investing in Kids and their Needs

Virginia A. Krolczyk, D.M., Ed.S, LPC

SPECIAL THANKS

I wish to express my sincere gratitude to Kathy Weinhart, a student of mine from Siena Heights University. She believes so strongly in the cause that she graciously proofread the book in its entirety noting edits that needed to be made. I am extremely grateful for her skill, time, and encouragement. Together we hope for change.

"The book is great and I hope that someone that can make a difference will read it and help to change the system. I will be praying for that to happen."

~Kathy Weinhart

DEDICATION

This book is dedicated to Brennan, Alena, Viveca and Jax. May the wisdom you gain, by being active in your learning, always guide your decisions. Cherish, appreciate, and share your knowledge, patiently, since insight and understanding is one of the greatest gifts one can offer.

I would also like to dedicate this book to my husband, Kenneth; for without his love, support, encouragement, and wisdom a draft to final copy would not have been possible. Thank you for all your patience and understanding while fulfilling my passion of writing.

Counselogy Concepts

Washington Township, MI

Manufactured in the United States of America

ISBN 978-1-387-27147-4

2nd Edition

Student Capital

Table of Contents

CHAPTER 1

A NATION DIVIDED

"America is a nation in crisis because American citizens allow it to be"

~Dr. Krolczyk

What Happened?

Many people do not understand the severity of chaos that exists in society today. Citizens live in an era where technology is at an all-time peak, data spearheads curriculum, information is easily accessible, and kids do more sooner. However, despite these advancements parents feel inadequate, kids worry about their future, teachers are demoralized, and leaders in schools are frustrated. Additionally, employers describe numerous skills that are lacking in this generation of workers. What is causing this model for disaster? This is the prominent question asked by numerous politicians, state legislators, school officials, and employers across the nation.

Student Capital

State and federal boards are scrambling to find a solution, but have yet to define the problem.

The reason the problem is so difficult to identify is because there is not just one cause; multiple factors have led to kids shutting down from society. For one, insurmountable pressure is placed on school systems to fix the problem; yet a school system in and of itself does not create the problem. The functioning of the school is only one facet of many that has led to the downward flow of educating today's youths. If this problem is going to be addressed then all aspects of a student need to be considered; including parenting structures and mental stability.

Reestablishing the whole child concept needs to be a priority so upward learning can occur. Too much pressure is being placed on young adults and as a result they are on information overload. Not knowing how to process all this information, they become extremely overwhelmed and begin to lose interest. This lack of motivation is misconstrued as not caring when really the student is simply trying to understand the purpose of the process.

Dr. Krolczyk

There are too many disconnects between education and society which is why all the strategies being put into place do not work, and won't work, until the separation between expectations and reality is bridged. Humankind needs to understand that people connect with students, not programs. Furthermore, current graduation requirements impede on career technical education; which is what the nation is experiencing a shortage of. A factor constantly overlooked is educators being inundated with data and paperwork; thus taking time away from teaching youths. When new tasks are added; former tasks should be removed.

To further exasperate this disconnect is the distinction between the technology used in industry and the technology used in schools; it is not always the same software. Aligning skills taught in the schools with skills needed for the workforce can alleviate a large percentage of anxiety experienced by young adults. These are just some of the systematic flaws that have caused youths to either cheat or fail; both of which leave students feeling unaccomplished. Pupils will never be prepared to achieve unless staff members are afforded time to work with them. The *on the job training mentality* needs to be transferred to the culture of learning. When the correct resources are not available implementing a plan is meaningless because that plan will be ineffective. For example, even if all kids had access to all programs; educators need to be available to help transition students to these programs. Another click, another link, another website will not elicit students to want to learn. A professional persuading a student to try their personal best because that professional believes the student has the ability to succeed is what will inspire a young adult.

The biggest barrier in education today is kids do not have the desire to learn. The reason that desire is nonexistent is because school is not fun. Schools are not creating engineers, mathematicians, or scientists. Consequently, schools should be preparing kids to think like these professionals. Graduation requirements need to be reevaluated so as not to stress kids out. Youths are refusing to come to school and because of this do not receive information on career options, identification of high paying jobs, or opportunities offered to disadvantaged students. Policy makers need to listen to students and educators on why absenteeism is so high and invoke change. Connecting kids to programs begins with getting kids to school. Too many troubled kids go unnoticed because there is not enough staff to dedicate time and attention to these young adults.

Students are not associated with learning because they are required to obtain a certain amount of credits to meet graduation requirements. Most of those credits are designated by the state, and some local school districts have additional requirements on top of the state ones. Few of those credits are electives which mean on a daily basis hardly any of the classes a student takes is their choice. This inability to have options inhibits student capacity to build upon strengths and stay focused.

A student is therefore expected to sit through school, all day long, listening to subject matter and lectures that they have little to no interest in. As if that is not bad enough, then they have to go home and try to remember what was taught and complete a lengthy homework assignment on it. So much nonsensical homework is being given in academic classes because there is a misconceived notion this will make kids smarter. Since the majority of classes a student takes are academic, this type of thinking is preposterous because kids are swamped with assignments they find meaningless. It is not realistic to give a bunch of homework on a subject some students have little to no interest in and think they are going to gain some great insight from it.

A student receiving a high school diploma may not be prepared to embark upon the world and all the mayhem that exists with it. Unfortunately, there are not enough career counselors in the schools to offer students the guidance they need when taking classes or exploring interest. School systems continue to invest in software programs and upgrade technology, yet neglect to devote the capital to hiring more staff to ensure students understand these programs. A paradigm shift needs to occur where school systems are actually dedicated to student capital™ and it is the aspiring young adult which reaps the benefit of student success. When a business invests in it workers, the company flourishes because those workers in turn take care of the customers. When a school system invests in students, those students feel valued and become contributing members of society. Value is something that is created, not bought.

Student capital is about developing young adults; finding out what is at the heart of their soul and bringing it forward. Increasing student capital is about increasing student connections and helping them understand not only *why* something is important, but also *how* to achieve it. Kids need demonstrations of *how* to complete things so they can feel assured the direction they are taking is accurate. Staff members need to be afforded the opportunity to develop and nurture relationships with kids.

Students need individualized care and guidance. This feat can be accomplished one of two ways: give staff members less responsibilities so they have time to devote to students or hire more staff members to share in the increased responsibilities so more time can be dedicated to students. The bottom line is by spending more time getting to know students a greater sense of trust will develop which can lead to a better understanding of their needs. Addressing these needs can lessen stress and anxiety. The problem is no one realizes this.

Educators do not have time to foster relationships with kids because they are inundated with creating and filling out forms for accountability. There is only so much time in a day and if the majority of it is spent on bookkeeping, little is left for instructing. Every time something "new" or "additional" is rolled out, teachers honestly do not know how they can ethically commit the attention to perform the task accurately. Any effort put into something new takes away from currently existing processes. That is to say if a new strategy is supposed to be better, it should replace the old, not be added on as extra. The problem is, no really knows if the new approach will be better, so they hold on to both. This type of strategy is hollow and becomes confusing, thus widening the gap between education, life skills, and careers.

Importance of Knowledge

The lack of knowledge a person has to function on a day-to-day basis is comparable to not having enough information about a disease; if the disease is not treated properly, it will become more widespread. Eventually, it could inhibit a person's overall functioning. This is the best way to explain the crippling effect encompassing this millennium generation. These young adults go through the motions of everyday life without commitment, passion, or drive. They exist in a world where little to nothing is required of them, so they function with nominal effort. Responsibilities, chores, errands, and tasks are not expected.

Even if they are told to complete such deeds, little to no consequence exists if tasks don't get done; therefore human behavior has been conditioned not to exert time and effort when completing things. Such a mindset allows lots of opportunities to immerse in the wonderful world of electronics; gaming, binge watching shows, viewing or creating videos, and visiting multiple social media sites. Instead of acquiring insight, knowledge, and great wisdom of the world in which they live in, these young adults have capabilities in technology, and well, that is kind of it. However, for their existence that is good enough because the adults around them praise how wonderful and talented they are for having those technological capabilities. They receive accolades for doing what comes natural to them, without any struggles or hard work.

Millennials think all this praise is great until they get accused of being dumb, lazy, and selfish. How did a society of more educated adults raise less educated children? Several factors play into this American educational crisis. For one, kids maneuver technology with such grace everyone is in awe of their capabilities. So much they can't wait to brag about it, advertise it, and base a child's overall value from it. The reason adults are so impressed is because a lot of what kids do, adults can't. Therefore, the kids of today are viewed as experts, highly diversified, tech savvy, and masters of electronics.

Since the millennium generation possesses such great skills in technology, they are bowed to and highly respected almost to a point of default. Regardless of how good their technology skills are, what is necessary to thrive and sustain happiness is still missing from these young adults lives. This misplaced happiness is causing problems for the individual emotionally, for employers when hiring, colleges when soliciting potential candidates and for families that yearn to create a structured balance in their household. Basic functions of pleasure that are detrimental for life are being overlooked and this oversight is wreaking havoc on society because schools have mistaken abilities in technology for accomplishment, parents have been misled to believe that if a student receives good marks learning has taken place and college advisors incorrectly trust students that take rigorous classes in high school are smarter.

Students graduating high school are not prepared to acclimate themselves in society. This is because while in high school students sometimes do not realize that a test requires knowing the material and this involves preparing, reviewing, and understanding the information to demonstrate proficiency. If a student has a short attention span in class, dislikes school, or cannot keep up with the pace of educational expectations that student will struggle in school. When a student struggles continuously throughout the day that student shuts down. When the student shuts down, they don't come to school. Students' not attending school has become a real challenge for districts. The solution is not going to a different school; it is breaking down the information into smaller parts so it can be retained, processed, and utilized. Students fear the incapacity to keep up with fundamental learning because the essential factor of groundwork prior to mastery is missing.

There have been times when I have shared my knowledge and experience at seminars and others have commented "wow, you are so smart." I have had to reflect on this because I came from a low income household, raised by a single parent, was an English learner, had an attention deficit, and was a first generation college student. I often wondered how I sustained the ability to acquire and share knowledge when the odds were not in my favor. I realize it was not intelligence that drove me; rather, passion. I was interested enough to want to research various topics so I can obtain more information. Anyone is capable of doing this if they first understand their method of learning and type of personality. Personality traits drive interests, and interest drives learning. For these reasons a person should take a personality test, learning style assessment and interest inventory so they can have a more in-depth understanding of personal characteristics, process for obtaining information, and enjoyable themes. These three factors should determine individual career paths.

Unbalanced Society

Students make mistakes as part of development and growth and these failed efforts encourage learning. However, society has become so sensitive to student error that a slip-up can be detrimental to future endeavors. An example of this is when a student acts immaturely and it comes across as offensive, but not necessarily harmful. If the offended party files charges said charges could remain on a person's record for a long time thus inhibiting opportunity.

For instance, if a student "moons" another student, this act can potentially be considered "sexual harassment," causing the student that engaged in the conduct suspension, possible expulsion, and legal ramifications. That student is now labeled, scarred, and emotionally distraught for engaging in a childish act. The punishment does not fit the crime. Telling students "it's ok to make mistakes" but then when a mistake occurs condemning the action certainly sends inconsistent messages. It doesn't take long for students to figure out it is not ok to "fail" or make a "mistake" because there will be severe consequences when they do. This is when students become extremely paranoid about making any type of error. In such a paranoia state, they are less likely to take risks. Organizations are so concerned about lawsuits for not acting on reported issues; they have resorted to overreacting on everything reported.

Most administrators conducting an investigation of this type do not comply with Title IX rules of being "impartial and unbiased" and try to bully or threaten the accused into admitting things that perhaps did not occur thus fulfilling the obligation of completing a report that satisfies the offended party. However, by doing so the individual rights of the accused are possibly comprised through an inadequate investigation. The improper handling of a very serious allegation could create a hostile learning environment.

A one-sided investigation lacking proper due process could derail the accused of educational pursuits.

Investigations of this nature are occurring more and more because if a student's feelings are hurt, it is considered bullying. If a student is offended, it is considered harassment. If a student is uncomfortable, it is diagnosed as social anxiety. If a student lacks interest, it is an attention deficit. If a student is annoyed, the student needs anger management. If a student sees a psychologist, a plan is created suggesting the schools alter conditions for learning.

Perhaps the pendulum has swung too far whereas numerous youths are being diagnosed as having a mental health condition incapable of handling common life events. Today's youths perceive having your feelings hurt or being offended, uncomfortable, disinterested, and annoyed as abnormal conditions of life in need of clinical intervention. Parents seek medicine to help ease unfavorable emotions in young adults. Historically conventional medicine was contrived to treat diseases by providing comfort to a patient while the physician focused on understanding and correcting the problem.

There is a misconceived notion that when a youth experiences an unpleasant situation it is a morbid condition equivalent to an infection. On the contrary, an infection arises from a genetic or developmental flaw, toxicity, insufficient nutrients, or microorganisms transferred from one person to another. Negative feelings which are unavoidable are usually manifested by verbal expressions, attitudes, or behaviors and should be managed without medicine. Drug intervention suppresses a person's mood thus interfering with the ability to cope. The focus of comprehending unwelcomed feelings as a means of correcting them is nonexistent in treatment. To assess normal functioning as abnormal and induce altering thoughts through substances is unethical because emotions are necessary for human development.

The general public was shocked when a doctor was treating patients for cancer and those patients did not have the disease; yet society appears blinded by the fact that teens are treated for mental thoughts that do not constitute a disorder. Chemotherapy to a noncancerous patient can be damaging, subsequently prescribing drugs for beliefs based on perceptual experiences can also have adverse effects. Psychological treatments should include remedies to understand and manage painful feelings, not suppress them.

Hurtful experiences not dealt with can manifest into anger causing a person to act out. Medications disorient a person from the process of dealing with emotions hence making it easier to avoid feelings. Being derailed from experiencing feelings allows adolescents to think typical emotions human beings are supposed to experience throughout life constitute a mental incapacity and this type of thought process is very damaging to an individual and society.

Feeling Accomplished

On-going efforts need to be put into place so young adults can build and sustain a balanced, happy life which will offer them a competitive advantage. This includes nourishing their mind, body, and soul. The mind is their learning; which can be accomplished through reading, figuring out equations, critical thinking, and solving problems. The body is taken care of through nutrition; which includes exercise, good eating habits, meditating, and attention to hygiene. The soul is nurtured through spirituality; comprised from faith, belief, devotion, and trust.

When equal aspects of MIND, BODY, and SOUL are present a person reaches a harmonious sense of balance which provides confidence to inquire, socialize, and create. Life will be viewed with self-assurance, buoyancy, and purpose. Kids need this balance in their life; especially if suffering from severe anxiety or depression. Students have reported that once they acquired a balance between the three elements, they feel better. This same concept applies to adults too.

When the scale of mind, body, and soul is tipped too much one way and not enough of the other, despondency prevails. A person spending too much energy on one aspect of the model and not enough on the other components can cause a person to be in a bad place. Spending 4 hours a day at the gym everyday will make a person's body feel good; but not necessarily their mind and soul. The same is true of someone that spends all weekend studying; the mind may be nourished, but not the body and soul. Similarly, a person that continuously does for others neglects their own needs.

Dr. Krolczyk's Model of Accomplishment (MoA)

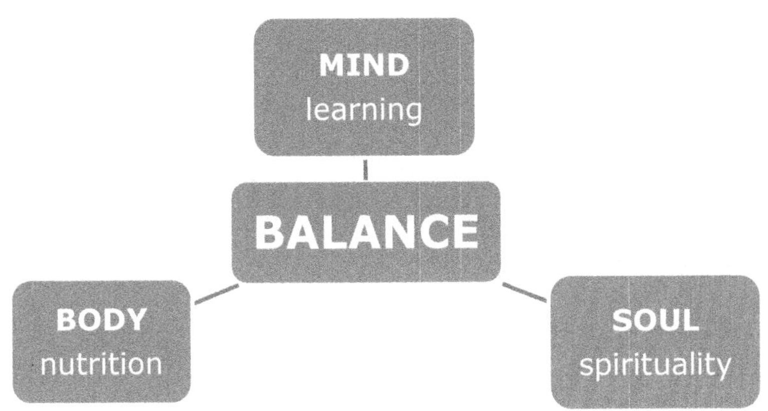

The key element of the MoA is to take a person from where they are at in life and determine what is needed to find this balance. This process of course will be different for each person since personal experiences vary. One person should not compare themselves to another person because each life tells a different story.

An example of this is someone that is a good cook. This person might aspire to move on from cooking to baking. Someone that doesn't cook or bake may want to learn culinary skills by starting with simple recipes, then as they become better explore more intricate ones. Someone that has reached a mastery level of cooking might aspire to open their own restaurant. The point being everyone can have problems balancing their MoA and that is ok. What is not ok is complaining about something you are not good at, yet doing nothing to improve upon it. For example, a person that doesn't know how to cook, nonetheless wants to learn to cook, however never tries to cook, may have difficulty fulfilling the stages of the MoA.

Learning entails developing a knowledge base of something a person does not already know. A new skill, awareness, a process for doing something differently; it involves a prospect that interests a person and they achieve a level of understanding. For example, solving a math problem, knowing the definition of a word, grasping the functioning of the human body, clarifying motion and energy, realizing the impact of input and output, putting together something, harnessing a garden, perfecting a recipe, knowing how to play a sport, drawing a design, hooking something up electrically, or mastering technology; these attributes all lend to learning taking place in different forms, on various levels and is individualized.

Regardless of what someone is trying to do, a person feels accomplished once the concept of what they are trying to achieve has been grasped. When a person's mind is not engaged they become bored, and boredom often leads to depression. Continually cultivating the mind with new and different things is a critical component of the MoA. This is why many senior citizens do puzzles or crafts; to improve brainpower, enrich memory, and create purpose.

Nutrition is important because when a person takes care of their health, they feel better. People who gorge on junk food usually end up feeling awful. This is because eating is also individualized, and some foods do not process well with some people's systems. Going back to the food chart, having a balanced diet serves a role in the operation of the human body. So when people get busy and neglect their eating habits they are interfering with this process. Yet something so important should be made a priority.

Eating well can be quite costly, so too can medication, therapy, and tutoring. When a person eats better, they tend to be more focused and have clearer thoughts. Exercise and meditation are known to release endorphins in the body, which make a person feel good. It also helps a person stay in shape; when a person looks good they tend to feel good, which is also why hygiene is so important. Cleanliness inspires an individual, and it does not take much to wash clothes, shower, wear deodorant, and brush your teeth. Neglecting basic needs is detrimental to a person obtaining their objectives. Feeling worthy and being able to concentrate helps people reach their goals.

Spirituality is the personal beliefs people have. It can involve religion, but doesn't have to. Some believe in a higher power or higher order and they look to that for guidance and direction. They pray, attend ceremonies, join groups, and act in a manner that is righteous. They instill these values into their youngsters which motivates them to behave in an ethical manner. They perform acts of kindness, good deeds, and engage in community service.

Inner pleasure is derived from helping others and such gratification encourages people to make morally sound decisions. This virtuous feeling allows a person to be less critical of themselves and less judgmental of others. When spirituality is present, a person develops a conscience that inhibits them from harming oneself or another. They sleep well knowing they have engaged in behaviors that were helpful, rather than hurtful, and arrive at a place of inner peace. When this part of the model is missing, people tend to be jealous, become resentful, and at times even hostile. Envy makes people angry and anger can become destructive. Faith can conquer anger.

The **MIND, BODY**, and **SOUL** directly relate to emotions and feelings. People that are in distress, in a bad place, unhealthy, spiteful, sad, or bitter have not found the momentum to balance the three. One aspect of all three needs to exist for a person to feel exalted. Once a person has found this balance, then it takes continuous effort to maintain it. People that are looking towards others to validate their happiness will never find it.

The only way a person is going to reach a level of stability is if they do something to acquire it. Taking care of oneself can be laborious, which deters many people from trying. However, this is what is required for a person to reach a level of jubilation. Therefore, if one is not willing to put forth the effort, then one should not expect **TO FEEL ACCOMPLISHED**.

When people indicate they can't find time to exercise, or educate themselves, or even get out of bed; what they are really saying is they are not ready for change. Until they are, nothing anyone else does will matter because transformation is self-induced. It is difficult to help someone who is unwilling to help themselves.

It is an undeniable fact that people want change; however change requires action, so it would be unrealistic to expect change without doing something differently. Making a commitment to alter a routine takes perseverance, desire, and patience. Without the presence of these characteristics, change is unlikely to occur.

Best Practices

Reflecting on companies that are successful and companies that are not, there are always patterns that exist that lead to the success or failure of a company. One of the configurations for a successful company includes investing in the employees; which is known as human capital. Prospering companies demonstrate that when employees feel valued, those employees work harder and are more likely to go out of their way to service customers, which ultimately benefits the company.

To further illustrate this point companies that are successful listen to what customers want. For example, when a cosmetic company asks women what they are looking for in a product, and then creates that precise product to meet woman's desires, that company will be more successful than one that creates a beautifying product and tries to convince women they should use it.

Generally, a lot of methods schools implement are illogical and are based on assumptions rather than facts. For instance, I had a student that was diagnosed with Oppositional Deviant Disorder (ODD). I was given a behavior plan to use that entailed therapeutic measures with the student involving a lot of actions for the teacher to take when the student acts out. However, teachers barely have time to instruct; let alone implement numerous procedures outlined for just one student.

The schools should not be treating the condition, schools should be aiding in integrating a student into the classroom setting. Kids need to be more respectful, resourceful, and responsible, yet programs implemented do not seem to invoke these types of changes. Teachers seldom are asked their expert opinion or professional thoughts when models of change are created. Such a dysfunctional process is creating an unhealthy environment for student achievement which colleges and the workforce are starting to notice.

Another illogical method in the educational industry is too many outside companies that do not consist of educational experts have created applications and software and are convincing schools this is what is needed for student success. Very few of these companies have had input from educators or students yet offer the assumption they know what is best for a field they have no expertise in.

To further exasperate matters, educational leaders continually tell students how to learn without ever listening to why they aren't retaining knowledge. Schools push careers on students without knowing which career a particular student would be best suited for. Practices of this nature are very similar to companies that have failed. If schools continue in this direction, more will fail and less will succeed.

In elementary school students are told traits they need for middle school. In middle school they are told what they need for high school. In high school they are informed of what they need for college and in college they are prepped for the work force. They get to that career and realize it was not what they thought; they don't have the skills they need, and the income is different than expected. That student is now an adult feeling unaccomplished.

Peers are powerful so when others hear this student did everything he was told he should be doing and still failed, students start to distrust the system. This isn't any different than a person using a make-up product exactly the way the sales representative explains they should, and not getting the results promised. That customer expresses their displeasure and other customers become apprehensive of the product. Society has become apprehensive of public education because too many ineffective models have been put into place.

To truly invest in kids involves inquiring what their needs, wants, and passions are. Too much pressure is placed upon the educational system to acquire data and most of this data is manipulated and meaningless. Data analysis is meant to drive instructional practices but if the data is not accurate, practices identified to prompt student learning will be ineffective. An overwhelming amount of stress is placed upon teachers to gather data through excessive testing which makes a teacher feel rushed so students are given answers without talking, explaining, or discussing the material. The students may remember the answers for the exam, but are at a loss when it comes to application and theory.

Students need to be thought of as clients and those clients need to be serviced. People that service student clients need to be treated with more respect. Teachers are so undervalued; they fear engaging in any activity that is not test related, part of their evaluation, or technology embraced. Even though a teacher may have a keen sense that the current structure is not working in educating students, teachers continue to engage in convoluted instructional methods because they are told they have to. A looming threat of increase in funding for technology and decrease for personnel has precipitated the issue of lack of student learning causing it to be sugar coated rather than handled.

Another critical default in society is the lack of connectedness available for youngsters. When kids feel connected to an adult; either a parent, relative, teacher, counselor, administrator, hall monitor, coach, secretary or custodian they have less absences, perform better in school, have more confidence, and develop a sense of trust. When they do feel anxious or depressed they will usually turn to this person for help in creating strategies to manage their stress. I actually had an associate principle tell me once to "spend less time with kids and more time on paperwork," which is backwards thinking.

Student Capital

A shift in the allocation of funds in school systems needs to take place making sure professionals are easily accessible to help nurture the spirits of young adults. Many schools have outsourced custodians, cut counselors and crammed kids into overcrowded classrooms. School leaders assert these actions are necessary to save money, yet spend excessive amounts of money on computer software programs or electrical devices. Furthermore, while teaching staff is being cut, bonuses are often given to central office administration. Better structures need to be put into place so school funds are not mismanaged.

The school culture used to consist of a community where everyone worked together and focused on the best interest of students. Many custodians lived in the area, coaches had kids that went to the same schools where they coached, and teachers had parents and siblings that were also raising their families in the same municipality. Neighbors knew each other and collaboratively kept neighborhoods safe. People looked out for each other and took care of one another. When schools decided to outsource or fire individuals that had long standing allegiances to the schools, communities became divided and started attacking each other rather than helping one another. For most school systems it was not so much a loss of revenue that contributed to cuts; it was more a shift in how money was being spent. The end result was less connectivity with kids and hence began the era of increased teenage depression and aggression.

Since parents fear their child being in a depressive state, they give them whatever they want and do everything for them. Doctor's seem to write prescriptions for kids that appear to be in distress and these kids being highly medicated seems to validate to parents a child is incapable of doing anything. The doctor and parent write a note to the school asking to collect homework, lessen assignments, and make tests easier.

The student stays in this crippling state of mind because they have not accomplished anything; on the contrary everyone has just made everything easier. Schools used to implement a sense of balance focusing on the whole child concept which transitioned well-functioning kids into confident adults whom took great strides to maintain a sense of happiness. Now, the focus is strictly academics and assessments, which lead to a false sense of success. This is because grades are inflated, test scores are not accurate, and students are declared unhealthy which causes them not to feel good about life. Teaching staff is so busy they do not notice a student that doesn't feel good about life. That is, until something drastic happens, like a school shooting or suicide and then the blame is placed on mental illness, not lack of infrastructure.

The competiveness in industries places a strong burden to strive for continuous improvement which adds value to their output. In manufacturing, it is not human resources, managers or engineers that are necessarily adding the most value; rather it is the press operators, saw cutters, and machine operators because these people make the parts. When cuts are made in industry, in most cases the employees that add the most value to creating the parts are usually the last ones to be let go.

The reason America is facing an educational crisis is because they want to run a school like a business, but they don't follow the business mentality. The added value in a school system is the teachers, counselors, and coaches whom have direct contact with students and the most opportunity to invoke change. Education differs from business when reducing staff. In education, the employees that add the most value to student achievement are the first to be cut. What happens in manufacturing when press operators, saw cutters, and machine operators are cut? More than likely, less goods are produced which impacts the overall functioning of the company. In education, when people that are front and center are being cut, less learning is taking place which impacts the school system as a whole.

Schools need to implement programs of developing all aspects of the child, not just one component. When only one portion of a person's well-being is addressed, they are disproportionate which causes aggression, fear, and uncertainty. This lack of balance makes it difficult to find enjoyment. So much pressure is placed on kids to participate in a rigorous curriculum and score high on assessments that teachers and students have dedicated all of their energy to just that and forgot how to have fun. In some instances, students have given up altogether and stopped coming to school; which ultimately has adverse effects. Students need to take classes that are appropriate for their level and they need someone accessible to help them determine which classes those might be. They also need courses that are interesting and pleasurable. Core academics all day long are not exciting for anyone. The end result is usually a failing grade, feeling of hopelessness, or misconduct; all of which could have been avoided if options and guidance existed for the student.

Students used to have choices like orchestra, radio broadcasting, or home economics which led to employable skills. They took classes that were meaningful and learned skills that would sustain them. The hands on experiences they would get from industrial classes, like how to use a measuring tape or read a ruler, were far more beneficial in careers and everyday life than solving complicated mathematical equations. Yet schools inundate kids with algebra and calculus and disaffirm basic mathematical principals.

Furthermore, students used to be allowed to make mistakes, and were encouraged to learn from them. Now, every error appears to be detrimental to graduation and their future. In short, this is another factor in kids not wanting to come to school.

Schools need to be more diligent in tracking and accounting for student's presence. This entails if kids are not coming to school, finding out why or what is going on. It has become too easy for kids to stay home and parents to call them in. There is a direct relationship between student performance and attending school. When kids miss school, they get behind and expecting the teacher to catch them up is unrealistic, so teacher's end up just excusing an absent student from everything missed.

This doesn't help the child, but the encumbrance of learning is too much for just the teacher to weather. If a doctor writes a note for a student, the parent calls in excessive absences, administration does not address policies, guidance counselors have caseloads at capacity, and the child is uninterested in attending school, what else is a teacher supposed to do? Unfortunately, implications of this type of behavior can have adverse effects.

Student Capital

What happens when that same child that barely attended high school decides to go to college and misses valuable instruction? Will higher education give the student a refund on their tuition? More than likely not because learning is not a money back guarantee. Learning is an essential function of life, nevertheless seems to be a burden not worthy of the time and dedication needed to reap the benefits. When a person gives the impression they can cook, when really they can't, they may starve. When a person gives the impression they know something, when really they don't, their ego suffers. Impressions are hollow and offer nothing more than a false sense of being.

Most colleges do not have an attendance policy, so if a student misses class it is up to the student to get the notes, work, and information needed pertaining to tests and grades. Most students do not learn well on their own, so being present for lectures and discussions is helpful in understanding the material. College professors are not interested in talking to parents, even those that feel it is their right because they are paying for the education. Professors take the position that "your child is an adult and you need to speak to them if you want to know what is going on." This is why students should be taught to be independent sooner, rather than later, so it is not such a culture shock when it happens.

Consequences come with independence and that is ok. Allow students early on the opportunity to fail so they can learn from that failure. Resources and tools are made available to students in high school and college; it is up to the student to utilize these resources to enhance their learning. If they don't know how, then they need to ask. I am astonished at how many students have reported feeling anxious over having to order food or ask a question. These actions are viewed as contributing factors to having a panic attack.

To put it mildly, a basic task such as ordering food should not lead a person to have a complete meltdown whereas they have to see a therapist and possibly become medicated. This is actually happening more and more, which makes one wonder if a person has a severe reaction to mild situations what will they do when tragedy really strikes? How is this person ever going to survive anything if basic executive functioning skills are not present? This is why learning how to talk to others is a must and if a person chooses not to, well, that is their choice and they have to deal with the effects of it. However, as they mature and grow they may make different decisions based on outcomes of previous ones.

All things considered, kids have too large of a safety net, which is why attention needs to be refocused on reinforcing attendance policies. Many schools have polices, but they appear to be continuously overlooked. Stronger guidelines need to be put into place to ensure that does not occur. Attendance issues should be a priority for ever school leader. A high school student will never be able to master the curriculum if they are not present or active in their learning.

Passing these students along the system only causes greater grief at a later time. Measures taken at an earlier date can have better long term results. In some cases, parents are seeking additional support or reinforcement from the school. One parent wrote, "I noticed a trend towards increasing absences, tardiness, and missing assignments. At what point does the school take action in the form of detentions or other method of reprimand? I am humbled to admit we have had our struggles with our child and need the schools support." Specifically, stronger measures for attendance need to be put into place and accountability on the schools and parents should be clearly outlined.

It will take a culture of dedicated citizens that are willing to invest in student capital that will elicit the necessary transformation for a more promising future for this generation and others to come. This book will help manage the direction society can take so youths can fundamentally and educationally flourish. Once kids excel, anything is possible.

Amidst mounting challenges, a child can be cultivated into a confident, wise, courageous, and caring adult; all of which are characteristics of a strong leader. When people focus on the aspects of a life they love, they are happy. When emphasis is placed on things they hate, they are miserable. Outcomes become a reflection of choices made and if people want different results then they need to make different choices.

CHAPTER 2

THE EDUCATIONAL DOWNFALL

"People often mistake increased activity for increased achievement"

~Dr. Perry

Communication Obstructions

There exists a belief that to obtain information faster, better, and easier a menu of options needs to be present. Broadening a network of online tools appears to be the means for accommodating this. While this concept sounds good in theory, the reality is it doesn't work. An influx of activity does not equate achievement.

Many organizations have the mindset that by referring customers to information online, the company is being innovative. Virtual information has become so convoluted people are simply turning away, thus causing businesses to lose customers. The industries that are able to sustain success are the ones investing in customer service; personable, face-to-face service.

The same thought concept applies to schools. Parents and kids alike are discouraged because an abundance of information is being thrown at them at once and none of it is being explained. School leaders sense they are being efficient because so much literature is available in so many places, but it has become overwhelming, confusing, and time consuming to seek out. On the verge of exhaustion, families have stopped looking and accept the fact that pertinent information is going to be missed.

The schools blame the parents for not being more involved, the parents accuse the schools of ineffective communication, and in the end it is students that miss information pertinent to success. Students not realizing they exist among a broken system begin to feel inadequate leading to heightened anxiety and depression. Parents sensing they have failed their child compensate by coddling them. Since students lack information needed, teachers appear insufficient. The response- an increase in the amount of material being delivered; thus starting this vicious cycle all over again.

Student Capital

Effective communication is not about how much information is given, rather the delivery method used to portray the most important aspects. For example, bullet points or highlighting significant details is more likely to be read and remembered than jumbled paragraphs or multiple pages of literature. It has almost become a contest to see which school doles out the most information; so many newsletters are filled with details that do not pertain to every student. Therefore, a parent needs to skim through the letter in its entirety to determine what applies to their child and what does not.

Many parents are working parents and don't have the time to decipher excessive amounts of information. If a parent has multiple kids in different grades then there are multiple newsletters to review. If each schools newsletter is 25-30 pages long, and a parent has kids in high school, middle school, and elementary school then that parent could be reading close to 60 pages a month just to find out what is going on in the children's schools. There exists a structure in education that is flawed when it comes to communicating.

The same model is occurring with student's college applications and applying for financial aid. The process has become so involved, kids are shutting down. The college's solution is to increase the amount of information available for students on the college website, so much that it has become muddled and kids do not know where to begin. I often hear "kids are smart they will figure it out" or "these kids are so tech savvy" but what people forget is these kids are also human and as human beings we often need to see the value in how our time is being spent.

When a person has to work that hard to just locate the college application, then has to go through various tabs to find out what programs the college offers, the cost, scholarships, athletics, and more, that person becomes exhausted by the time one school is researched. Everyone is quick to assume the student is just being lazy. I have often found the student is more baffled by the process and feels a sense of frustration because everyone expects them to know how to do it. A simple process has become way too complex and no one is giving these kids the suitable guidance they need.

Student Capital

The reason applying to college has become so difficult is because nothing is straight forward anymore. What I mean by this is when a student clicks on a college website; the application is not in clear view. A student usually has to click on future student, and then undergraduate admissions, then create a log-in, and then apply. Every link they clink is flowing with more and more links to more and more information. If a student doesn't realize future student or incoming freshman refers to them, then they don't' know where to begin.

Think about this for a second though. How would a student know? Who tells them? The teacher whom is being evaluated solely on student test performance? A school counselor that has an enormously large caseload and the majority of time is spent on administrative or secretarial tasks? The parents who are just as confused as the student? Or the principal that is always in the classrooms conducting teacher evaluations? I revert back to a systemic flaw and lack of investment in student capital.

Students are confused and need guidance and this is a huge problem in the public schools. A catholic school has a student-to-counselor ratio of 1-35 or 1-50 and those kids are given excellent guidance and direction in pursuit of college and careers. Comparatively a public schools student to counselor ratio can be anywhere from 450-1 to 650-1, in which case the majority of students are neglected causing extreme confusion when it comes to guidance and direction in pursuit of college and careers.

I frequently hear "what GPA do I need to be a doctor?" A grade point average in and of itself is not sufficient. Especially since most grade points are not truly reflective of a student's knowledge base. A student needs to be immersed in the process of learning and once they find their niche they should explore careers options.

Usually patterns unfold of certain subjects a student tends to excel in. The reason they do well in these subjects is because they are interested in the topic. Knowing how to apply what they are good at involves guidance. Professionals need to be available to assist these young, curious minds. Helping students build upon their strengths can be motivating and inspirational to the student and educator.

Student Capital

Lately, there has been a big push for equal opportunity for students, meaning low-income or minority students are being swayed to take advanced placement classes because the belief is they do not know about these courses and the benefits. Believe me, I am in the school setting talking with kids daily, and I can tell you the reality is none of the students know much about anything. There is too much information and no one is available to help them sort through it. Personal connections no longer exist and kids don't listen when information is given to the masses.

Kids need connectivity and if given that, they will start coming to school and everything else will fall into place. Time needs to be afforded so professional staff can make this happen. The only way to make time exist is to take away some of the current pressure and burdens. Relationships are a process, not something that can be forced or fit in. Once relationships are developed, they need to be fostered otherwise they will dissipate which almost defeats the purpose of creating them.

Dr. Krolczyk

Students enter high school excited about the social aspect. The prospect of attending college or creating a future post high school is far from their minds. The primary focus for most students is on lunch time and classes with peers. They know for the most part that they need to attend school and do well, but they don't see the true value of how a good education can impact them. They don't understand that the knowledge base they are obtaining, method in which it is being delivered, and significance of retaining such information can sustain them later in life.

As one parent stated to me, "My daughter does not get the importance of high school in relation to real life, so she isn't even applying herself." Due to this lack of appreciation students have found ways to manipulate and beat the system. Until a student is able to relate the context of what they are doing, to the existing world, learning will have little to no meaning. If learning has no meaning, neither will homework. Students will simply just go through the motions without any active engagement.

People often confuse value with cost. Value is a mindset that occurs over a person's lifespan; cost is how much you pay for something. Value is created, not bought. Just because something costs more does not mean it has greater value. Until society changes their views, the economy is going to spiral down impacting not just this generation but many to come. Leaders of today have to work diligently to bridge the gap between education, careers and life skills. Instead of waiting for humanity to crumple, governing bodies need to build, foster, and maintain relationships with the public sector to address ongoing concerns.

This means a huge educational reform, one that is needed desperately. Seeking out and partnering with the communities will enhance results when putting theory into practice. A lot of schools say they do this, but very few actually do, which is another reason there exists crisis in education; a plan is only as good as its execution and the execution of a plan is only effective if it is relevant to the needs of the organization.

Once again, one of the major issues in high school education today is the lack of guidance and advising with students. Pupils are clueless on what classes to take in high school. It has been beaten into their brain that in order to get into college they all need advanced, accelerated, and honors classes. Even though this is not true, there has been such a big push for this, those students and their parents think it is the only way to compete and be successful. Therefore, they sign up for as many of these advanced classes as they can, comprising their GPA and eventually having a complete meltdown because it is just too much to keep up with.

The student desperately wants to be able to manage all of the workload, since once again, that is what they believe is needed for college, so the parent out of concern for their child contacts the teacher requesting amendments of what the student has to complete. The teacher then fears due to all the adjustments needed to be made for so many students, the knowledge base of the material is lacking, so the teacher starts giving students the answers to reflect positive academic performance.

The student does well, the teacher looks good, and the parent is happy. Now it is the college that is confused when the student is unable to recall or process any of the material that was theoretically learned. This is one reason why a student that receives a high mark in a rigorous course is in need of remediation at the college level; grades can be deceiving.

High school is supposed to provide a solid foundation from which higher learning can build upon. That is no longer happening which is why so many colleges have students take corrective classes, stay in college longer, or end up dropping out altogether. The knowledge base a student needs to have to be successful in college has become limited and many higher learning institutions are teaching courses with subject matter that is very basic which is causing a delay reaching collegiate level standards.

Many students are not invested in the material they are learning because they do not understand the purpose it serves. Students often express, "when am I ever going to use this information?" or "why do I need to know it?" Many students have also indicated not doing well earlier in high school, which impacted their overall grade point average, which results in less scholarship money. In a desperate attempt to make up for this, they overindulge in classes they assert will boost their GPA; not taking into consideration the enormous workload that accompanies this decision.

A lot of software companies have created videos to accompany educational material so student learning is fun or entertaining, and are surprised when the student doesn't use them. That is because they are missing the point, if a student doesn't like history; a cartoon on it isn't going to change that. However, meaningful projects and conversations with peers and adults could sway thoughts and thinking.

People tend to remember things they do. That is to say watching a funny video isn't going to increase their knowledge base, but acting out a part of history or creating a timeline, or having in-depth discussions on the relevance of what they are learning will jog a memory when it comes time to apply the material. Students need to be engaged in learning and listening to a lecture or watching something is not active engagement.

Students often need examples to follow on how to complete assignments. I once witnessed a student-teacher debate. The student was insisting that he needed samples to complete the project. The teacher was adamant that if these were provided, it would sway the students thinking and he wouldn't offer original thought. The student maintained that an example would illustrate the process/format and the work would still be his own.

When I interjected and asked the student why an example was so important, he explained he wanted to be confident he was doing the project correctly. He further explained that one time he put forth a lot of effort into an assignment only to learn he was off base. When given the opportunity to re-do it, he was burnt out from all the time and energy he originally devoted that he couldn't muster the ambition to do it again. He did not want to make that same mistake. Sometimes what students need to learn makes sense, but no one invests the energy or time into asking them their thoughts and actively listening to their rationale.

Being told how to complete something isn't the same as being shown. Perhaps a better way to utilize support sites would be to have the site available as a reference for students that need further guidance. If the site contained outlines, practice tests or sample projects a student may find it useful. Forcing students to utilize technology sites will discourage them, but having websites available as a reference shifts the responsibility back on the student. Once students start using these sites as resources on their own, they will tell their peers whom will also start using the sites to aid in learning. It will become a practice students will believe they started when really it was strategically planned. The outcome will be students being accountable for their learning. This is a brilliant tactic in achieving a much needed goal.

The educational curriculum has taken a toll on student learning and must be adapted. 20 years ago, students had more flexibility and more options in class selections. Students are individuals and forcing all of them to take college bond classes isn't working. Rather, it places undue stress on everyone in the educational realm. Too many students are failing classes and using up elective options in their schedule by having to make these classes up. Furthermore, 20 years ago students were permitted to leave school for lunch or have half day schedules. This is no longer permitted and students are going crazy staying in school all day long with all academic classes. What is asked of these students to do most adults couldn't do; which is one of the big reasons kids are shutting down and not coming to school. Students are restless, bored, and need a break.

Too Much Homework

So, I have this theory and it goes something like this: teachers give too much homework. You see, most of the classes students take are academic and classes of this structure are notorious for giving homework. A student may spend so much time making sure the homework assignment is completed correctly; little time is left to do other schoolwork, thus causing a student to fall behind in other subjects. Multiple homework assignments add up causing extreme stress.

Students are under a lot of pressure to complete work outside of school and this gesture is taxing on a student's general mental capacity. Students struggle with completing work for subjects they are not good at. Some courses students are never going to get better at because they do not like the subject matter; so they will put forth as minimal effort as possible.

Dr. Krolczyk

Students have often reported "homework is useless" or "homework is a waste of time." These statements allude to the fact that young adults see little to no value in work having to be done outside of school. One of the reasons for this is because the homework seems to be "busy work" rather than something that will offer insight and purpose. It is time consuming, boring, and not offering any great insight.

One student stated, "I spend 7 hours a day doing work in school then I am expected to go home and do more; that's just crazy." The reason it is absurd is because students suffer from what is known as attention saturation. This is when the brain is exposed to something numerous times, yet does not recall specifics. Constant exposure, interaction, and use do not necessarily lead to accurate recollection; rather, frequently seeing something contributes to general based memory. Even though the capacity of the human mind is significant, remembering precise facts can be difficult.

When the brain is saturated with too many facts, it subconsciously determines details are not important. When students are exposed to material over and over again, it does not guarantee they will retain it. This can be why so many students struggle with tests. Exams are detailed oriented and details are not what the brain is good at.

For example, try to identify precisely the back of a $10 dollar bill. No matter how many times you have seen one, could you state exactly what is on the backside? More than likely your subconscious mind noted this piece of information as irrelevant and didn't transmit it to the cortex. Students are expected to know so much information, neuro transmitters are on overload causing information to get jumbled. This supports the argument that more elective choices would be refreshing for the brain. Oh, and by the way, the U.S. Treasury Building is on the back of a $10 bill.

In the early centuries, a Confucius professor conducted a psychology experiment asking students to draw a circle with one hand and a square with the other at the exact same time. None of the students were able to construct either one accurately hence showing when doing things simultaneously neither one gets done correctly. Multitasking never worked; yet more and more schools systems resort to it as a means to get "everything they have to do" done. Do less of something but do it accurately, and a person would have more success. I think of exercising; many trainers posit it is much better to do fewer pushups correctly, than more incorrectly. Shouldn't that came concept be applied to educating kids?

Doubly important is students have been conditioned to believe that appearance has more worth than substance, which is why so much energy is placed on getting high marks, even by cheating. Educators and parents are naïve to the epidemic of students cheating on school work. It is occurring across the board in all disciplines. For the most part, everything a student tells me is confidential.

For this reason, they tell me about their cheating. Based on an analysis of copious conversations I have had with multitudes of students, I have concluded the majority of students are cheating. While school leaders are trying to force learning communities in the classroom, students have formed cheating communities outside the classroom.

Student Capital

Restating the obvious, the homework load is cumbersome and most teachers are too busy to check it. Thereupon students use this to their advantage. Students take pictures of tests, change names on papers, pretend to be sick the day of an exam then take it later after being given the answers, fake anxiety/ADHD to take a test in a quiet secluded area which no one usually monitors, goggle answers, take pictures of worksheets and send them around, write anything down just so an assignment looks completed, and take pictures of a study guide, send it to their digital watch, and use it during an exam. Students have found these tactics to be creative, stress relieving, and necessary.

In any case, students are reporting significantly higher levels of anxiety, depression, and stress-related problems than they have in the past and research indicates "there is a current mental health epidemic affecting students and their school success" (Michigan Department of Education, 2017). With this in mind, legislators should pay attention to the correlation between state mandated pressures and student stress and anxiety. Especially since students aren't working on things that matter to them, so they feel unfulfilled and this can result in negative behavior.

When students work on things they care about, they see the importance in what they are doing/learning and are happy. According to the Michigan Department of Education (2017), suicide rates have increased by 40% among teens and youths and from what I understand, Michigan is not alone in this statistical rise, "the overall U.S. suicide rate rose by 24% from 1999 to 2014" (Tavernise, 2016). Government officials should be looking at reducing symptoms of depression and anxiety by first understanding what is causing it. Increasing more mental health facilities doesn't solve the problem, it only masks it.

Transitioning from High School to College

High school aged students have been told if they want a prosperous income they need to attend college and receive a degree. Obtaining a bachelor's degree once made up a smaller percentage of the population, where opportunities were only available for those with higher socio-economic status, but this has since changed. More people from different upbringings are now acquiring a bachelor's or master's degree. Even with a higher educated society, looming concerns about job prospects still exist. With more people attending college, there is more competition in the job market.

Having a college degree no longer makes a person stand out. So people over engage in other things to build their resume. By being active in so many things at once, people are becoming burned out. There is also the misconception that just by obtaining a college degree a person will be marketable; however if the degree is in a field that isn't growing, there is no market to seek. This is why I have created a list of questions students should be asking.

QUESTIONS FOR ANY STUDENT TO ASK COLLEGE REPRESENTATIVES

The best way to invest in student capital is for the student to manage the assets

~Dr. Virginia Krolczyk

1. What programs/degree paths does this college specialize in?
2. How do I determine which program should be pursued?
3. What is the student to teacher ratio?
4. What percentages of professors are fulltime?
5. Does the college offer professional learning communities?
6. Are there study abroad opportunities and if so, how are students informed?
7. Is this college affiliated with internship programs?
8. Upon graduation, does the college assist in finding a job?
9. What percentage of students have defaulted on student loans?
10. How does repayment of a student loan work?

Student Capital

11. What is the best way to position myself for a return on my investment?
12. What types of scholarships are available and when are the deadlines?
13. Are scholarships given automatically based on merit or does a student need to apply?
14. What is the deadline to fill out the FAFSA?
15. What is an award letter?
16. Is someone available to help understand the award letter sent by FAFSA?
17. Does a student need to reapply for scholarships and FAFSA each year?
18. How much is each credit hour?
19. How many credit hours make up one class?
20. How many credit hours typically is a bachelor's degree?
21. Is tutoring available?
22. Are professors available outside the class?
23. What activities/groups/organizations are available?
24. What services are available to assist students educationally and emotionally?

Dr. Krolczyk

Numerous times students have applied to colleges and checked a box on the application that they didn't understand. Different forms of admittance have different meanings and can be detrimental to being accepted. It is critical students know and understand the various types of the admission process prior to applying.

Some of the terms a student may see on a college application include rolling admission, early action, early decision, and regular decision, deferred/waitlisted, weighted GPA, cumulative GPA, recalculated GPA. Students also confuse undergraduate vs. graduate, community college vs. university and transfer student. These terms need to be reviewed with students so they have a clear understanding of each. Essentially, this is another reason why counselor caseloads need to be smaller.

Students tend to think their grade point average does not count for second semester because the valedictorians and salutatorians are identified after first semester. This is a flaw in thinking because it does count, most colleges ask for an end of year transcript. When a student struggles in a course and wants to drop it second semester, they should check with the perspective college they applied to and possibly have been accepted to.

The reason is if the college asks the school to send an end of the year transcript, and if the student did not notify the college of a class change, this can be viewed as being dishonest and comprise their admission. A student never wants to get caught in this scenario so it is always best to air on the side of caution. Each college has different guidelines for admittance. Additionally, a student should not bail the first sign of trouble; figuring out how to persevere through challenges could prove very beneficial.

Ideally, schools should have staff members that specialize in areas of advising. For example, one person designated to handling FAFSA, another person for college applications, another person for skilled trades and certifications, another one for scholarships, a different person for AP classes and college, one person for graduation requirements and credits, and even one person designated to handle mental health concerns.

If that is all that this person is responsible for, they will become an expert in that area and also have the time to properly advise students. Unfortunately, schools don't do this, so people and information is scattered and kids are advised in groups where some of the information doesn't pertain to their educational pursuits. In the end, kids are on information overload and staff members are so busy they do not have the time to help kids sort it all out and aid in designing a foolproof, individualized, post high school plan.

CHAPTER 3
SCHOOL PERSONNEL

"Education is the most powerful weapon which you can use to change the world"

~Nelson Mandela

Respecting Teachers

Teachers are being asked to provide data, research, and evidence of student learning. By spending an enormous amount of time gathering all this information, there is little time left to prepare and teach lessons. Teachers are so busy trying to prove students are learning, they aren't actually teaching them. Instead, they are giving students the answers so they perform well on standardized tests.

The data becomes manipulated, the teacher appears effective, and the student continues to struggle because they never learned how to get the answers, they only knew what they were. The entire process of learning is missing. More and more educators have resorted to this method for survival. This is not what students want or need, but such a complicated structure exists, they have become prey to it. Furthermore, pressure is placed upon teachers to pass students that haven't completed any work.

Accountancy does not equal efficiency; many schools can look good on paper, but the data can be convoluted or flawed. If a school district is going to attest that it is really investing in kids, then it should do it. This can be demonstrated by imparting value on students where learning experiences prepares them to take on further challenges after high school and become exemplary citizens of society.

It also means sharing a vision with staff. No matter how great the plan is that exists, if employees don't buy into it, success is limited and any action put into place will become another thing to "check off" a list thus lacking sincerity. Teachers need to understand the purpose of a plan and be afforded the opportunity to contribute to the overall process. Distributing leadership to teachers can aid in implementing effective strategies.

Student Capital

In brief, too much emphasis is placed on teachers to make the class fun and entertaining that the teacher becomes stressed trying to figure out how to make the class material amusing. The teacher quickly realizes it is easier to give students answers than to expect them to engage in learning. Some teachers can put on a bright yellow costume and sing and dance and it still might not be enough to engage a student in the subject matter and somehow that becomes the teachers fault.

Teachers are under so much scrutiny, they fear deviating to anything unstructured and instruction becomes monotone. Certain subjects may not be stimulating to some students, so they quickly drone out the teacher's lecture. This is why students should be afforded the opportunity to have choices on courses taken and teachers should be allowed the flexibility to instruct without additional accountability. Teachers also need more control in the delivery of instruction so innovation can occur naturally.

A teacher is a highly educated expert who spends a lot of time with students and understands what methods work best for teaching and learning. Seldom are they allowed to explore strategies based on observations. Instead, a principal with less experience, less education, and less time spent with kids is telling the teacher how to conduct their lesson and then evaluating the teacher on it. How does this process make sense to anyone?

When companies bring in leaders with less experience and less knowledge it affects sales. When schools bring in leaders with less experience and less knowledge it impacts kids. Teachers are so stressed because it has become impossible to meet the demands incessantly placed upon them. They have overcrowded classrooms, constantly changing curriculum, mandated testing, continuous emails, and few breaks.

Every class period they are performing and being rated on that performance. As if that is not exhausting enough, they are expected to go home and check papers, check emails, create lessons, and research better teaching strategies; all of which takes time away from being with their family.

A profession a person used to go into for the love of the job has now become unmanageable with unattainable goals. When people with less background and experience working with kids make decisions for people that do work with kids, it creates a model for disaster. When a parent is burnt out, it affects the entire household. When a teacher is burnt out, it affects students.

The majority of students want to learn the material and would rather the teacher interact with them and elaborate on lectures; but time does not permit for this type of engagement to exist within the confinements of the classroom. One student explained, "The teacher was so funny when explaining information that when I saw it on the test I thought of the teacher's humor and remembered what was said."

Another student commented, "Projects in class help me remember things, for example in German we draw and color maps or make advertisements for food using videos or posters, the visual representation and act of creating is very helpful when recalling information." An elementary student stated, "I remember all the continents through this real cool song my teacher taught us, and we have another one for the parts of the human body."

These examples are the kind of instruction that have lasting effects. I wonder how often kids have been asked how they retain and process information so it has meaning to them and once this information is obtained, how much of the curriculum is structured so techniques highlighted can exist? This process seems appealing for any school that wants to acquire true success.

If school systems do not commit to a strategic investment in kids, learning will never take place. For example, anyone who takes time to exercise on a regular basis reaps the benefits of laborious efforts. It's all about the process and commitment. A person may not always be in the mood to engage in strenuous activity, but continues to put forth the effort of working out because of the pledge they have made to acquire better health.

Pet owners share the same philosophy; people who own animals take the time to teach them right from wrong, how to behave, and how to respect people and things. The animals that comply are rewarded with affection and offer warmth back. Kids are no different; they need guidance, redirection, boundaries, and assurance, which of course involves attention, strategy, connectivity and a lot of patience. In return, they are humbled, grateful, independent, and balanced.

This is what every educational institution should strive for by allowing teachers the freedom to educate youths based on the teachers expertise of what works and what does not in regards to students retaining information. This form of management is known as distributed leadership which is different than shared leadership. With distributed leadership, the person the task is doled out to has total autonomy. Micromanaging is not part of a distributed leadership style.

If a class is reading a book like Lord of the Flies and the teacher decides to incorporate playing survival games, splitting the class into tribes, and having student competitions where the winning group gets breakfast or a government teacher presents mock cases with simulated trials, teachers should be commended, not reprimanded. Students attest this style is the most meaningful and remembered because students are actively engaged in the process. The visual representation helps them to understand the material.

Dr. Krolczyk

There are numerous theories on what should exist for quality teaching to take place. In essence, how many of these theories have input from students themselves? Regardless if a student is considered at-risk or high performing, based on a student survey, students have reported similar practices when they feel quality learning is taking place. These include:

project based assignments
smaller class sizes
completing work in the classroom
reviewing and checking homework
examples given and explained
student questions answered, not redirected

Sadly, very few of these processes are embedded during class time. This is mostly due to the excessive amount of standardized testing that exists in the school systems today and the direct relationship student performance has on teacher evaluations.

Legislation posits that students achieve significantly greater learning from teachers ranked highly effective and pupils lose ground to peers when taught by a teacher categorized as anything less. A teacher is evaluated from an administrator and must demonstrate growth in learning; which is an increase in test scores. Millions of dollars have been spent on observation training so a principal, whom visits a teacher's class twice a year, can offer helpful feedback on how a teacher can improve in the classroom.

While the system was set-up to offer support, it has instead had the opposing effect. Teachers teach to the test and spend little time on anything else; seldom is meaningful feedback given to teachers from administrators because, once again, most principals have less educational experience than the teacher being evaluated. Furthermore, a teacher whom spends the majority of time with students is being directed by a principal whom spends little to no time with students on how to instruct their class. Nothing about this process is in the best interest of students.

Consequently, this is not the only issue with student instruction. Students need to procure personal mastery which is where a person learns by doing. Taking action to apply oneself, practicing what is learned, and striving for continuous growth will help develop habits that contribute to an overall sense of accomplishment. This is why teachers need to have boundaries in the classroom. Boundaries help students establish good habits. When a teacher outlines conditions pertaining to grades, the teacher needs to adhere to those conditions and students will eventually conform and stop making excuses.

The issue with this is teachers are not always supported. If a parent complains or makes unreasonable requests, school system leaders give in to this because they do not want the student to go somewhere else and risk a loss of funding for that student. Due to financial greed, quality instruction is being compromised.

The parent is not the educational expert, the teacher is, and giving in to such demands is not always in the best educational interest of the student. Rather than respect a teacher's professional stance, parents continue to argue for the sake of their child being happy; at least that is what they think. Eventually this practice has a spiraling effect because true learning was sacrificed so the student feels unaccomplished hence impacting happiness.

With that being said, there will always be exceptions where students should be accommodated, but those circumstances should be few and far between, carefully evaluated and monitored, and only instituted when absolutely necessary. The ideal educational structure exists when teaching kids is at a level that is appropriate to their maturity and capability. This allows students to fully grasp the concept before moving on to the next level. State mandates have robbed kids of this component.

The content and manner in which subject matter is being taught is not conducive to every students learning style and to keep passing students through the system without fixing the underlying issue is an injustice to society. It's like an auto company that makes car parts, if brake pads are not being produced properly, but the goal is to get as many made as possible, in the quickest amount of time, then workers have reached their goal.

That is until the brakes are installed into the cars, end up defaulting and recalls are made. In some instances fatalities occur and a public statement is made apologizing to the public. This rushed process in the end causes the company more time, money, and aggravation.

Conversely, that is exactly what is happening with education, at a student's expense. Students are rushed through the curriculum to get through as many subjects as possible in the shortest amount of time, and when they go to college or enter the workforce they are defaulting. The educational structure they lack is recalled through remedial courses, but unlike the auto industry that takes responsibility for the error, the educational system allows the student to take the blame for the rushed process and if the student feels worthless and kills himself, no public statement or apology is made because no one is willing to accept the system is part of the problem.

An auto company does not blame the driver for brakes defaulting, yet the educational system considers students the culprit. Just as interesting, if the student is not to be blamed, then the teacher is. This systematic error has wreaked havoc on the educational system in this nation.

Student Capital

Some of what goes on is beyond a teacher's control. However, there are some measures teachers can take to make the flawed process smother. For example, teachers need to understand that giving a ton of meaningless homework is unrealistic. Students are inundated by rigorous curriculums that exhaust them; adding more labor to that is mentally draining. Students remember more by being involved.

A social studies class having teams and acting out the trench warfare is more meaningful than reading material and answering questions that perhaps do not even make sense. Just because kids are having fun doesn't mean they are not learning. Sometimes less is more and giving less homework, reviewing that homework, and developing relationships with students so they feel at ease asking questions is when real learning will take place. When that happens, students will start scoring better on assessments and become less anxious throughout the process.

When students are less anxious, they apply themselves more, which will help alleviate some of the stress teachers feel. Many teachers are experiencing health problems derived from strained working conditions, extreme pressure, and overbearing parents. Such health issues are causing teacher absentee which impacts student learning. If a student is going to acquire personal mastery, a teacher needs to be in a sound state of health to help guide the process.

Another reason kids shut down is they get so far behind they have little hope of catching up; so they give up. Too many students have reported being absent and upon returning having so much work to make up, while trying to stay current, they are completely overwhelmed, stressed, and exhausted. Initially one would think "oh-well, too bad, deal with it," since all these millenniums ever do is whine and complain, right?

Wait a second, if anyone has ever had a child home sick, or has been ill themselves, then they know the last thing you are able to do when you don't feel well is complete arduous tasks. Sometimes professional judgment needs to be made and in certain circumstances students need some reprieve. Now, I understand this can get complicated at times, but the truth is if so much homework wasn't given all the time to begin with, a student being sick or out for a day or two wouldn't set them so far behind that they felt they couldn't recover.

The statute of the American educational system has become quite sad; even elementary students are up late completing assignments. These are kids that should be playing and having fun instead of being hassled with constant school work that needs to be completed at home.

A colleague of mine continually reminds parents increased activity does not equal increased achievement. If someone thought giving kids more homework makes them smarter, they are completely wrong; instead it adversely impacts their mental health placing them at risk for burnout, major anxiety, and depression. Some homework of course is feasible, but like everything else in education homework has been taken to a whole new level and kids are given mass amounts to complete on a daily basis. It is discouraging, impractical, and unlikely to contribute to providing a sound educational baseline.

Due to all the pressure in schools, some students' emotional state is being compromised. Anxiety disorders are occurring at alarming rates and at very young ages.

The goal of becoming leaders in the nation needs to incorporate frontrunners in mental health incorporating strategies for therapeutic measures with adolescents.

Intervention and prevention tactics are needed now in schools more than ever before. Thus answers the question of why kids today are so "angry." If you worked all day, then worked all night, day after day, eventually it would take its toll on you and you would be irritated too. School work should only be sent home when it is meaningful, necessary, and the teacher intends on reviewing it the next day for accuracy.

If time does not permit for this then homework should not be given. Otherwise it is a complete waste of everyone's time because kids are rushing, not paying attention to detail, cheating, and many households have parents that work so much they are exasperated trying to figure out the assignment while balancing dinner, laundry, bills, and other children. Unless there is a purpose to the assignment, don't give it. Once upon a time, homework was meant as a means to "practice" what was learned in school; but it appears less learning is taking place in school, therefore less practicing is needed.

If a teacher truly wants to be effective, they need to ensure kids learn the material before they have them practice it at home. Otherwise, once they get home they are going to be completely confused. The "practice makes perfect" concept only works if they are practicing the skill accurately; otherwise bad habits are formed. Also, they have to be the ones practicing it, not the computer or a parent.

At the beginning of every school year, parents post all over social media the need to prepare for the bombarding of homework parents will end up doing because it is too complicated for their child. Yes, parents, and the reason for this is the student doesn't always understand how to complete the assignment, nor does the parent, so time is spent at home trying to figure it out or at least arrive at somewhat of an answer so the student can receive credit.

Interestingly, arguments manifested in 2006 that the average homework load had skyrocketed and this increase is hurting kids (Mathews, 2006), but society disputed such claims. Ten years later, homework is even more intensified and believed to be directly impacting a student's psychological state. Not only is the student's mental health affected, teachers are experiencing extreme distress.

Sometimes the curriculum is so complicated the teacher doesn't understand it, in which case the teacher is better off telling the student "I don't know" instead of giving the wrong answer. An incorrect answer is misleading because the teacher is the trusted professional, whose word is taken at face value, so being honest is the best way to establish trust. It is ok not to know something, but it is not ok to misinform.

A constant complaint of students is when they ask a question rather than get an answer, they get redirected. Students report being told "ask 3 classmates before you ask me" or "you should have looked at the website" and the all-time favorite "here's the link." I have gone to some of those links kids are given and the problem is, once they get there, they don't know what to do or where to go to find the information they need to complete the assignment.

Student Capital

I get it, teachers are overloaded and don't have much time for kids that are confused, which is exactly why education needs to be restructured. A pupil copying off another pupils work isn't learning, yet that is the culture that is being created with "so much to do."

Legislators assert there is no money for educational endeavors, yet millions, perhaps even billions is being spent on damage control, remedial, mental health, and technology. That seems backwards. It would be cost effective to slow down, have smaller class sizes, and ensure kids are learning. Just like a glitch in a product can cause a major manufacturing error, kids' not gaining knowledge is a major systematic error. The process in which they are being taught and curriculum they are exposed to may not be conducive for learning to exist. This flaw is causing youths to shut down.

So many aspects of education that served a purpose have been eliminated. For example cursive writing is not taught in schools anymore, and this component seriously needs to be brought back because it was an aspect of excellence kids used to work at; it was their signature, trademark, and identity. Currently, they don't practice it at all. Everything is completed on computers with spell and grammar check.

The millenniums vocabulary is horrendous because they are not forced to think or understand words on their own. I am shocked at how many basic words my own kids should know at their ages and don't. One of the reason kids are getting questions wrong on state mandated tests is because they don't understand what the question is asking. Words like "aberration" or "abate" are words that may appear on an exam and could completely throw the student off if they do not know the meaning of the word.

If they understood the connotation of these words, they may correctly answer the question. Kids don't read much anymore and this too has directly impacted their writing ability and vocabulary. Books read in school are not interesting to them, so they have no motivation to read on their own.

Helping Students

Students need to grasp the concept that the only way they are going to get better at learning, studying, and taking tests is by doing it themselves. My daughter's soccer coach doesn't ask me to practice soccer for her, so I am not sure why parents feel compelled to complete kids' homework.

I understand it does not start out that way; the parent is only helping, thus encouraging their child to complete the assignment. Once they realize how complicated the assignment can be, rather than write the teacher a note indicating a lack of understanding, parents enter helicopter mode and try to fix the situation for their child by completing the work for them.

While intentions are good, actions could inhibit progress. My daughter wouldn't improve her footwork if I was the one kicking the ball around, nor am I a soccer expert, so while I encourage her to practice, I trust she is practicing skills her coach taught her.

A child doesn't improve learning if the parent completes the assignment. It is always obvious when the parent does the work because the child doesn't know the material, yet turned in an elaborate assignment. Taking shortcuts doesn't make kids better, it puts them further behind. If the child doesn't understand the work, write the teacher a note and say so.

Parents often worry that the child will be accused of misconduct or not paying attention, which may or may not be the case, but the bottom line is if the child doesn't know how to do the assignment they need to learn it and need help in that process. If this becomes a continued occurrence, perhaps meet with the teacher to determine what could be going on because other factors might be involved. Discussing a situation with the teacher and blaming the teacher are completely different.

I recall my older daughter, when in fourth grade, all of a sudden coming home every day wanting help with math. Eventually, I got irritated and all I could think of is why isn't her teacher properly instructing her on how to do it. I finally inquired as to why she was so confused and the teacher was perplexed. She responded that not only did my daughter fully grasp the concept; she was always the first one done and went around the room helping others.

What the teacher and I discovered together was my daughter was attempting this feat of asking for help at home as a means of getting more attention from me and my husband. While this revelation was difficult to accept, it was necessary to implement changes so she didn't feel the need to resort to measures that did not accurately reflect what she was capable of. Once changes were made, behavior started to change.

What was critical in this scenario was working with the teacher, accepting constructive criticism, and enforcing a plan that addressed the issue. The teacher agreed that if there was a day she felt our daughter did not understand the assignment; she would email us so if she asked for extra help at home we would know it was sincere. This collaborative effort helped our daughter to continue to prosper in math.

In my daughter's case, it was important my husband and I got to the root of the problem because understanding the fundamental concepts of a subject matter is critical to build upon. This did not happen to be what was going on with my daughter, but is the case with so many other students. I had a student that cheated his way through Algebra I and when he got too Algebra II, he was completely lost. He frequently acted out in class and when the student finally admitted he just didn't understand anything, he was placed back in Algebra I and actually put forth effort this time learning the material because now he grasped how important the process of learning Algebra I was for going on to the next level.

Reshaping Guidance Counselor Functions

Most school counselors have the capability to direct and guide students, but are limited on time. Meaningful conversations need to take place about course scheduling, college programs, skill trade certifications, financial aid, and scholarships. Students need to be better informed on opportunities that exist based on their interests and performance.

Numerous conversations have taken place amongst school leaders on bringing someone in, like a temp service, to assist students or direct students to an online site; which eventually would prove ineffective. Experts exist in the school that can service kids but are bombarded with organizing and coordinating testing, lengthy paperwork, and administrative/secretarial tasks.

Counselors need to be relieved of these other duties so they are able to properly meet, connect, and guide students. The last thing a student wants is to be referred somewhere impersonal when seeking guidance. Re-directing kids and parents to online sites or links only shuts them down. They need someone to personally help them by answering questions on college, careers, the workforce, and varying aspects of mental health. Care and concern needs to be exhibited so students know they matter.

This is why the private school model works and the public school one does not. To be clear, when I say private school I am referring to a catholic school, not a charter school. Charter schools steal school funding without enforcing state curriculum and offer the impression students are knowledgeable when indeed in most cases they are not. I have yet to enroll a student from a charter school that is better versed than students in public schools. The reason the private school model works is simply due to the smaller counselor to student ratio. It makes sense and it works.

The comprehensive and guidance counseling model suggests a school counselors time should be spent on responsive services, individual planning, classroom guidance, future planning and system's support (American School Counselor Association, 2016). Zero percent of their time should be given to non-guidance activities, such as testing. Yet, the majority of a school counselor's job entails other duties as assigned; leaving little to be accomplished in the role a guidance counselor should serve. This directly impacts kids.

I have heard from many people "I never visited my counselor in high school," but for every student that didn't, there were others that did. The truth of the matter is some kids need more direction than others. However, this doesn't mean other students shouldn't be offered guidance; sometimes kids just don't know what to ask. This current generation of students is presented with more challenging and diverse situations, which complicate decision-making.

Student Capital

Schools are so focused on having kids exposed to careers and buying into a career path that student learning has been overlooked. Students' complete interest inventories to match their skill with their ability. Surveys of this nature are given to students starting at a very young age. However, interests and abilities change as youths explore life. Therefore, these inventories are not an accurate assessment of young adults' true capabilities.

Instead, give students a learning style inventory and personality test. If a person knows how to learn and what characteristics contribute to their learning, when they are ready to declare a path they will be able to maneuver this feat with great zest. On the contrary, if a person knows their interest, but not their learning style, they may not know how to acquire their goal. One must first know themselves before they understand how they fit into the world around them.

Preparing students for complex situations is critical to success. For example, social media has heightened bullying, many households have both parents working, divorce is more common, learning is much more intense, and job security is questionable. All of these pressures contribute towards excessive worry, stress, and concern. Not having someone to talk with to work through some of these difficult situations can be devastating.

Some kids hold things in, get to a breaking point and lash out. This is extremely unhealthy, dangerous, and debilitating. No one truly comprehends what is involved when helping a student work through social/emotional concerns. Many students of today's generation are paranoid, have a skewed sense of reality, and find communicating with others awkward. Regardless if these perceptions are accurate or not, a person becomes fixated on feelings to a point of delirium.

Building relationships with kids takes time. Once a relationship exists, counselors are able to better guide or direct students. I once called a senior down to discuss recovery classes and graduation, I had a little more time than usual, so I asked about post high school. This was when I discovered the student worked at a restaurant and helped with the cooking. He excitedly said, "I love going to work every day." When we discussed going to culinary school, he said, "I don't how to do that."

Clearly, this was a student that discovered a passion and needed more guidance. Had I never called him down to discuss credits he needed, I never would have discovered that. There are so many students like this one that never get the time, attention, and guidance they need.

The majority of conversations I have with kids are how to apply for a personal curriculum, test out of a subject, fill out paperwork for a flex option, how to complete paperwork for an early college program, what courses an approved career technical educational program can get them out of, basically, what credits they can use to count for other credits. The process has become so involved, all of my time is spent explaining it and no time is left just to get to know the students.

I was working with another student for over a year before she shared with me her brother died five years ago and her parents fight constantly. I was helping a first generation student with her personal essay when she told me she has a disabled sister she helps takes care of and has an after school job. Kids have a lot of "stuff" going on with them and finding out some of that "stuff" can be helpful in helping them create goals; on a personal and educational level.

I became a guidance counselor in 1999, right after the Columbine Shooting. This was the first of a series of school shootings across the nation. This historical event caused alarm and a heightened need for counselors in schools. A critical component that was lacking with the teens that committed the horrific crime at Columbine was a connection to someone; within the school or at home.

This connectedness could have helped these troubled young men work though thwarted feelings. Not surprising, suicide rates went down when more counselors were placed in schools. However, through the years, counselors started being cut or eliminated because situations in schools were under control. When more counselors were in the schools and available for students, the graduation rate was higher and school crime was lower.

Instead of heeding these statistics, schools decided to "find ways to do more with less." State leaders refer to this method as "thinking outside of the box." What they fail to realize is kids are not boxes; they are human beings with thoughts and feelings. Attempting to find different means to service children, without factoring in emotions, is a recipe for disaster. Allocating funds for school personal is investing in students because teachers and counselors are on the front line and could detect a problem before it becomes a tragedy.

The comment an associate principal made to me was asinine. The rationale that "more is coming down the pipeline" so "we have to streamline time spent with kids" is foolish. If anything, it should be the other way around. Since "more is coming down the pipeline" it is the "pipeline" that should be streamlined so as not to interfere with clogging. In other words, the paperwork should be simplified so more time can be spent with kids.

Student capital is about developing young adults; finding out what is at the bottom of their soul and bringing it forth. This is one way when counselors have professional development it needs to be meaningful. Vocational counselors were originally placed in schools to assist students with career choices, placement in the workforce, and becoming model citizens.

Dr. Krolczyk

Guiding principles were used to direct students' vocational development by helping individual students make high school a meaningful endeavor, and as a result, these students were better prepared for future aspirations. Counselors had the capability to work with students on personal differences hence expressing sensitivity towards their needs. Addressing trepidations helped a student adapt to the school culture.

Assessments were considered a valuable tool to address educational aspects of a student's life and create related goals. The reason these standardized tests were so significant was because time and attention was given to reviewing and interpreting the results for each and every student. The data was also interpreted for parents so they could make scholastic decisions in the best interest of their child.

The current model for school guidance and counseling allows little, if any, analysis of outcomes with parents. Mass emails are sent generalizing how to decipher scores causing befuddlement, fretfulness, and strain. All of this confusion trickles down to the student whom internalizes it. Kids are given explanations in large groups. No one elucidates to them how their score impacts them or what they can do with the information. Therefore, testing is perceived by students to have little, if any, relevance.

School guidance counselors sit in meetings that encompass teaching strategies, and attend workshops on improving test scores when they should be permitted to go to seminars that include self-injury, suicide, depression, anxiety, substance abuse, grief counseling, gender dysphoria, college admittance, and skilled trades. Money is never allocated for counselors to become better at what they do.

This baffles me since counselors play such a critical role in advising kids. To keep up with the ever changing times, counselors need to be current on trends. School systems need to do a better job supporting counselors on this endeavor. One of the core democratic values is the pursuit of happiness and counselors have a difficult time aiding students in this effort when they themselves are not familiar with current theories or trends.

In-servicing counselors on current philosophies and movements in society will help students reach their goals. Career development concepts have evolved over the years and counselors need to be acquainted with occupational expectations so they can better assist students with aspirations. The role of the school counselor in the schools needs to shift so it better aligns with the comprehensive and guidance counseling model originally set forth to meet increasingly diverse challenges students face in an ever-changing, global, technologically induced world.

Immediate attention needs to be given to the guidance kids receive and the platform in which school counselors deliver it so overall educational goals can be met. When Donald trump won the presidential election it shocked the nation. The media had to humbly admit there is anger in the country about the election results; anger also exists in education and the media needs to start listening to citizens so the same miscalculation on what the American people want and need doesn't occur.

Administrator: Leader or Manager

Large corporations sometimes as a desperate attempt to save money place less knowledgeable people in supervisory roles and since these people have less experience or education, they too are paid less. The problem with this mindset is when customers ask questions or want to know things; the supervisor doesn't have the expertise needed for the job and therefore cannot answer the question or help the customer out. So what does the customer do? Go somewhere where they will get better service and answers to their questions. Wherefore that same company that tried to save money by placing a less qualified person in a leadership role loses money and may go bankrupt.

Similarly that is what schools are doing; placing young, inexperienced people in principal roles they can pay less. The issue with this is they don't have a clue how to run a school and as a result, kids and parents are left frustrated causing some to go to other schools, become homeschooled, or explore other options like online schooling. Accordingly, an experienced teacher has little to no respect for the inexperienced principal and that quickly impacts the culture of the school.

Sadly, principals have become more like managers than leaders. Instead of offering great insight and wisdom, they oversee teachers to make sure they are doing their job. Very few principals in all my years of education have inspired me. In fact, lately, administrators have become discouraging, power hungry, self-centered and bitter.

Is this really the type of person society wants overseeing children's education? Instead of empowering teachers to achieve their personal best; they demoralize, attack, and instill fear. Teachers retire early, take sick leave, or change professions altogether because of constant attacks on their character, ability, and skills.

The teacher is viewed as a defiant individual and the principal sees their role as someone who needs to keep them in line. Except, this isn't the military, teachers aren't soldiers, and a principal isn't a sergeant. Anyone that goes into the profession of teaching is a very dedicated individual committed to helping kids learn and reach their educational goals. They deserve honor, respect, and praise for their sacrifices and devotion. In this case, if their own leader isn't willing to applaud their efforts, why would any member of the community?

Student Capital

Kids are smart and can sense when animosity exists. Just like in a divorce situation when parents are constantly at odds, kids know how to take advantage and manipulate the home environment. Comparably, the school setting isn't any different and when a building doesn't flow, student's figure out quickly how to benefit from that.

"I didn't do my homework because the teacher didn't give it to me" or "the teacher didn't explain that assignment," and now it becomes the teachers problem, not the kid who more than likely skipped class or was on their phone the entire class period. I am not sure when exactly education took a turn for the worst and the teacher became the enemy, but once it did, all of the teachers' energy became invested in defending him or herself against ridiculous allegations and little oomph was left to teach.

For some odd reason, society seems ok with the continuous attacks on teachers. By discrediting a teacher's level of education and professional opinion, a student is given total control. When a student is absent the day of an exam, the student decides which day would be good to make it up and informs the teacher.

If a student doesn't turn homework in when it is due, the student does it later and turns it in for full credit. If a student does not feel like coming to school, the teacher needs to make sure the student gets the work missed or are expected to exempt the student from the homework. If a student does not do well on an exam, no worries, a student can just re-take it.

These are the kinds of pressures administrators are placing upon teachers and such demands are ruining kids. None of these actions remotely resemble real life and when students are faced with situations where adjustments are not an option, they can't handle it. In other words, the increase in emotional outbreaks pre and post high school is directly related to students lacking accountability.

There is a concept in management theory known as "The Peter Principal" and for the most part this is when a person does well in their current position so they get promoted but do not necessary have the abilities for the new role. They end up being promoted beyond their skill level and eventually are unable to perform effectively.

Conversely, this is what is occurring in education with administrators and is contributing greatly to the collapse in education. A person may do well as a teacher or other staff member, and even though they have not yet acquired the competence for being a principal, they are still placed in that role.

They quickly become insecure, defensive, and frustrated with the different skills needed to fulfill the promotion. Rather than admit they are not entirely sure what they are doing, they make poor choices. The lack of confidence becomes evident and staff members lose respect for the person that is supposed to be their leader.

Their ego is inflated by being asked to be in this position, but quickly becomes deflated when others realize they have no clue what they are doing. Since they are in a position of power, they use it by tormenting anyone that questions decisions they make. Such incompetence sets the organization up to fail.

Educational entities need capable, confident principals that make decisions based on knowledge and experience, not conjecture for the purpose of appearing to have control. Some of the best principals I have seen have empowered staff to make informed decisions and supported them on it. When a principal wants to have control over everything, but doesn't know anything, decisions become a guessing game with a 50-50 chance of being wrong. Particularly, these are not the kind of stakes educational organizations should be taking with kids.

By and large principals come in, under qualified, and want to make their mark by changing things. There tends to be no rhyme or reason to the change other than they are now the boss and everyone needs to know it. This becomes annoying real fast. Teachers become disgusted with this prospect and usually stay out of the way; as far out of the way as possible meaning doing nothing extra, leaving immediately when the day ends, and using all their sick days. Accordingly, teachers don't inquire about things because they fear putting themselves out there.

Great opportunities may come up for kids and they let it fall by the wayside because they do not want to deal with the egotistical, under qualified principal. Since the principal is so afraid of making an error, they run every decision by upper administration. Central office doesn't want to appear as if they don't know the answer, so they make up one. No one considers the student, circumstance, or what may have been done previously; they run with what they think might be a good answer, yet this response lacks substance and could severely impact a student. The teacher fears reprimand and says nothing and it is once again the student that suffers.

I have seen numerous job postings where the job description of a principal is "The administrator will be expected to attend numerous school events, meetings, and classes, but will also need to attend professional development and school board level meetings as needed. A school administrator must be organized and well-versed in school matters.

A school administrator must also be understanding, yet diplomatic when dealing with parents, teachers, and students." For the most part, it is an individual that can work long hours. The lack of quality leadership in the schools has become a huge part of the American educational tragedy. Teachers are attacked for such petty bullshit they are afraid to make a decision, even if they know it is the right one. This will backfire on schools when a tragedy occurs.

Let's say for example a teacher hears an explosive sound in the building. The teacher knows the best action to take is to evacuate the students. However, no one has given the teacher direction to, the teacher worries about getting in trouble or being wrong, so the teacher keeps the students in the building.

Then another explosive goes off, this time impacting the classroom where the teacher considered having the students vacate, but didn't. Now it is too late. In hindsight, everyone claims the teacher would not have "gotten in trouble" for acting in good faith. Unfortunately, few educators believe that, because that is exactly what teachers are "getting in trouble for" and have been conditioned to not use their professional judgment to the best of their ability and for the safety of kids.

One change that can be made in the realm of leadership is better support of principals with the daily operation of a school building. If principals felt more supported by upper administration, perhaps they would better support their staff. Due to so many budgetary cuts, many school principals spend their time overseeing restroom supplies, classroom material, and picking up garbage around the school.

This is not the best use of their time, especially where visibility in the halls is more important than ever. Building relationships with students and staff becomes challenging when time is dedicated to custodial tasks. Principals need to be given the autonomy to create a culture that is warm and inviting.

Think of your own home and how much attention and detail is given to making it comfortable. The same personal involvement in a school will allow principals to increase capabilities and overcome challenges. This liberation will give them the courage to manage resources, perform tasks, and take actions that will lead to successful outcomes. Additionally, when principals create a spirit within the organization built on sincerity, accountability comes naturally. When a perpetual falsehood exists, staff members see right through it and lose faith in the system.

Historical in the business sector there were top-down, command and control, reward and punishment types of leaders. However, many companies found this style to be ineffective, costly, and slow. All things considered, contemporary approaches sought to empower individuals to participate in the developing of goals and sharing of responsibilities. Effectively, important tasks were carried out and for this reason companies achieved success.

Contrasting what has become known as best practices, schools chiefly exhibit dictatorship leadership style where as one or two people make all the decisions and as a rule expect everyone else to just carry out tasks. Very little recognition, reward, or encouragement is given and a lot of insult, chastising, and retribution exists. A highly educated individual is completely disregarded and not encouraged to be a critical thinker that can add value to the process.

Changes that have been implemented come from a limited perspective causing practices put into place to not accurately reflect student's needs. There exists a gap in education between the needing and acting and this gap continues to widen as people with limited knowledge continue to govern policy.

Student Capital

Likewise, many principals are not visible which can contribute to the heightened anxiety students are having. When a principal is office bound, students do not know who the principal is and this causes a lack of confidence in safety. By being present, approachable, and making direct eye contact a principal demonstrates interest, concern, and protection of the student body. This genuine behavior promotes a positive culture of the school and leaves an immeasurable lasting impression.

High visibility dispels rumors and encourages trust so students sense a safe harbor when attending school. Principals need to focus less on policy, practice, procedure, and protocol and more on rapport. Not everything is black and white; there are a lot of gray areas with students and families and the only way a principal would learn of those is through camaraderie. Decisions can be made in the best interest of kids, for each kid, if staff takes the time to get to know the kids.

After all, not only is what students are learning important, so too is how they are learning it. Generally, administrators should focus less on teachers and more on student outcome. A great deal can be detected through interactions with kids. Something as simple as greeting students when they walk in the door can build relationships that impact student learning. Successful educators make a concentrated effort to walk the hallways, visit the cafeteria, attend school events and listen to students. If a tone is to be set for learning, the person setting it should be familiar with what is happening in the school with first-hand knowledge through direct observation and participation.

Decidedly, students, staff, and the community are always watching and a leader being involved matters. So too does being kind. People easily detect when a person lacks sincerity. Principals should focus less on vision and mission statements being long, involved, and not a true representation of the school culture and instead, keep the vision and mission simple, easy to remember, and realistic. In the end, this is more genuine than the muddle most statements are comprised of.

Elect School Board Members Carefully

One of the most critical aspects of a leader is to ensure appropriate goals are set and met. As a consequence, leaders that view themselves as individuals that exert control over others have a skewed sense of authority. A leader creates organizational goals and a manager controls resources to achieve those goals efficiently. In short, the best way to inspire and motivate others is to govern policies together.

Both managers and leaders are essential to success, so complementing one another is conceptually the most practical method for closing the needing-acting gap. Coincidently, school board members are viewed as elected officials entrusted in governing policies that meet the educational best interest of students. As such, to oversee a culture of learning, a school board must understand and exist among that culture, beginning with interactions and conversations with multiple stakeholders as a critical component in addressing varying needs of students.

All in all, local schools boards need to be aware of social and emotional aspects of learning. This approach integrates academics with self-awareness, relationship building, and effective decision-making in an effort to reduce levels of anxiety and stress and develop a greater capacity and desire to learn. All things considered, members of the school board need to pay attention to what is going on within a community.

Are kids feeling burnt out? Are they being tested too much? What is essential for their learning and what is not? For the most part, creating policies that meet educational goals is not as simple as it sounds. Historically, constituents have trusted that if the board enforces an action it is necessary. But is it? Sometimes practices are put into place that cause more harm. This is why board members need to weigh decisions carefully, ask questions, and have a clear understanding of their population. In turn, the best way to service a population is to know about the population you are servicing.

Let's not forget the value of Administrative Assistants

Administrative assistants, previously known as secretaries, are extremely valuable to a school setting. These individuals take the time to know the kids, parents and staff. They are extremely familiar with policies, procedures, and forms. Normally, they are organized, detailed oriented, and efficient. Ordinarily, they are the first to be cut or let go. As a consequence of such cuts, work is doubled. Just like everyone else, they then have a difficult time keeping up with duties and responsibilities. This additional stress causes them to pay less attention and detail to matters. With this extra work load in mind, they tend to be brief and short with parents and students, offering a poor impression of a school.

I recall when my first child was born I was having a difficult time finding a pediatrician I liked. Someone advised me to stop and visit different doctor's office suggesting if at first glance the office is clean and the secretary is friendly, that means they are happy working for the doctor. In turn, the doctor must be a good person.

I originally thought this was ludicrous, relying on the demeanor of an assistant and cleanliness of a room to determine the quality of a professional. Specifically, how did these factors relate? However, over the years I have found this piece of advice to be crucial when seeking a medical practice. All things considered, when a receptionist is pleasant, there is no doubt the doctor treats her with respect. Likewise, he more than likely treats his patients with respect too.

Anyone can be a doctor, but not every doctor is a nice person. A patient deserves both, particular when ill. Additionally, receptionists that are enjoying their job tend to take care of the office atmosphere. Being similar in many ways, a school clerk can be representative of the school principal, which as a rule alludes to the overall climate of a school.

Much Needed Attendance Clerks

In the final analysis, schools need to be more diligent in tracking and accounting for student's presence. This entails if kids are not coming to school, finding out why or what is going on. To begin with, it has become too easy for kids to stay home and parents to call them in and coincidently there is a direct relationship between student performance and attending school.

For one thing, when kids miss school, they get behind and expecting the teacher to catch them up is unrealistic. Thereupon, some teachers just excuse the absent student from everything missed. This doesn't help the student, but the encumbrance of learning is too much for just the teacher to weather.

To begin with, when a doctor writes a note for a student, the parent calls in excessive absences, at the same time administration does not address policies, and guidance counselors have caseloads at capacity. This is coupled with an absent student lack of interest in completing work. In conclusion, a teacher is left with limited options when students do not attend school. Unfortunately, implications of this type of behavior can have adverse effects.

What happens if the child goes to college and misses valuable instruction? Will higher education give the student a refund on their tuition? More than likely not because learning is not a money back guarantee. Learning is an essential function of life despite lately being viewed as a burden not worthy of the time and dedication needed to reap benefits. When a person gives the impression they can cook, when really they can't, they may starve. Likewise, when a person gives the impression they know something, when really they don't, their ego suffers. That is, impressions are hollow and offer nothing more than a false sense of being.

Most colleges do not have an attendance policy so if a student misses class it is up to the student to get the notes, work, and information needed pertaining to tests. In particular, students do not learn well on their own, so being present for lectures and discussions is helpful in understanding the material.

College professors are not interested in talking to parents, even those that feel it is their right because they are paying for the education. That is professors take the position that "your child is an adult and you need to speak to them if you want to know what is going on." In summary, this is why students should be taught to be independent sooner, rather than later. Consequences come with independence and that is ok.

In the long run, kids have too large of a safety net which is why attendance clerks are needed. Many schools have polices, but they appear to be continuously overlooked. In any event, if attendance issues were the only focus for attendance clerks, many of these issues could get resolved. Attendance issues should be a priority for ever school leader and personnel need to be hired to help manage this. Subsequently, a high school student will never be able to master the curriculum if they are not present or active in their learning and passing these students along the system only causes greater grief at a later time. Clearly, measures taken at an earlier date can have better long term results.

In some cases, parents are seeking additional support or reinforcement from the school. For instance, one parent wrote, "I noticed a trend towards increasing absences, tardiness, and missing assignments. At what point does the school take action in the form of detentions or other method of reprimand? I am humbled to admit we have had our struggles with our child and need the schools support." In any case, what that support entails should be decided upon as a team, beginning with having a clerk available to arrange a team meeting. After all, school officials are busy handling multiple tasks and a situation like this will go unattended. Therefore, stronger measures for attendance need to be put into place and accountability on the schools and parents should be clearly outlined.

Dr. Krolczyk

The Argument for Hall Monitors

What precisely is a "hall monitor?" This used to be someone that sat at a desk in the halls, and as suggested, monitored the halls. This individual observed kids going in and out of bathrooms, hallways, classes, or even trying to leave the school. It was someone whom helped take note of kids and their actions.

At first glance, it may seem these people did not serve much of a purpose. Contrarily, they are very essential to the functioning of a school. Most schools have cameras, but these devices in and of themselves are not enough to discern student actions. Whereas having someone physically present is.

Students are going into bathrooms and breaking toilets, using substances, fighting, and engaging in all sorts of negative behavior. For the most part, they are getting away with it because there are too many students and not enough staff to keep track of these students' whereabouts.

For one thing, the more people present, the less likely students will be to cause such disturbances or damage. Furthermore, students knowing they are not being watched are more tempted to cause chaos. In the long run, schools can achieve more with the hiring of additional staff to help keep a watchful eye on these youths.

Custodians to Cafeteria Workers to Bus Drivers; Everyone Matters

Custodians and lunch workers are great assets to schools. These people tend to know a lot about what takes place in a school; especially with kids. They hear things, see things, and just know things. When hiring a custodian or cafeteria worker from within the community, more energy from this person is exerted in keeping the school safe.

I have known many custodians that were parents or grandparents of students in the school. These are the type of people that will go above and beyond typical responsibilities because they have a personal commitment to the community. At the same time, when schools cut these people and start hiring from temporary services, this permeates a different tone.

Employees hired outside the community are not as dedicated to the overall well-being of the students within the school. It is worth paying more to employ workers that have an invested interest. When bathrooms are not getting cleaned, soap dispensers are always empty, and dust accumulates this is a sign of lack of care and concern. However, if a custodian had a child or grandchild that attended the school they were cleaning, and that youngster had allergies, you better believe that school would be scrubbed from head to toe. See the difference?

Accordingly, treating people in these roles with respect is important too. Sometimes higher ups discount the arduous tasks of cafeteria workers and custodians. When employees feel undervalued, they tend to do less. At one of the schools I worked at the administration gave a holiday luncheon for the staff. When the principal walked in, he pulled a chair up and sat with the custodians. He could have sat at any table he wanted, but he chose to sit there. Knowing this, they felt special. Again, small gestures can bring great results. The same holds true for bus drivers. Hire from within the community and treat them like they matter. After all, the jobs these people do is so critical to the overall culture of a building, they deserve recognition.

CHAPTER 4
THE TESTING DEBATE

"Anxiety is derived from fear and people fear what they don't know"

~Dr. Krolczyk

Test Anxiety or Lack of Test Knowledge?

People often state when not performing well on a test that, "I am just a bad test-taker," or "I have test anxiety." While this may be true for some, it is not likely the case for most. Not that long ago I worked with a group of at-risk students and discovered most students that do not do well on an exam do not know the information. The vast majority of these students were not bad test-takers rather these students were just bad at taking notes, studying, and time management.

What I quickly discovered working with these at-risk students was most of the time little to nothing was done to prepare for a test. For the most part, a student might receive all A's on the homework which leaves parents and educators bewildered on why that same student does not perform better on tests. Parents especially are quick to accept the notion their child is just nervous when taking tests. However, after surveying numerous students I found just the opposite to be true. Most students that got all A's on the homework and failed tests cheated on the homework and did not study for the test. To summarize, they did not know the material.

All things considered, most homework now is checked for completion, not accuracy. Once students realize this, they are less likely to put forth effort and more likely to put anything down just to have the homework completed. They may receive full credit for having it done, but haven't learned a thing. When it comes time to take the test, the student doesn't have a clue about the material.

Contrarily, there are some teachers that do check for accuracy and students still perform poorly on tests. These students fall prey to the cheating epidemic that is occurring all over the educational industry. It exists through group chats via social media and students generally take pictures of homework and send it back and forth. To make matters worse, since most students did not complete the homework and questions aren't asked in class, the teacher thinks everyone understands the assignment.

Copying one another's work has become so prevailing no one is talking about it for fear of admitting a problem exists. Above all, students believe they are being creative whereas most teens are involved in so many things they do not have time for homework. Since teachers have so many concepts that have to be covered they have no choice but to send a lot of work home.

Another contributing factor to this cheating epidemic is parents working harder and longer hours thus causing them to have less energy to review homework. Likewise, much of the curriculum now is beyond some parents' levels so parents are almost relieved when their kids don't ask for help. As long as the homework is showing as completed and the student gets a good grade in the class, which directly impacts the GPA, everyone is happy.

Sounds brilliant right? Well, at least for a little while; until the student has to apply the subject matter. Once that occurs, they are doomed because they never really learned the material to begin with. Learning is a lot like calibrating equipment; close enough is not good enough and once this flaw is discovered it inhibits further progress until corrected.

Fixing it does not mean giving kids all the answers. When this occurs, all the student is doing is rote memorization which requires no analytical thought. Intellectual thinking entails the processing and application of information. Mastery is obtained through continuous practice. Americans are said to be behind in reading, writing, and math.

You cannot expect to become better at something you don't do. Reinforcement of reading is minimal, or simplified with videos and entertainment. Technological devices correct spelling, and math is taught at such high levels kids have completely lost interest or shut down. Kids don't know how to study because no one teaches them how; therefore, the end product, which is the student's knowledge base and ability to think critically, is jeopardized. The art of accomplishment is mastery of skill and as a nation the United States is not doing such a good job ensuring this is done.

Everyone always wants to fix things for kids because of such an overwhelming desire for them to be happy, only to later realize they are not happy because they never acquired a sense of accomplishment. Americans need to change their perspective and realize kids need hands-on experience to compliment theoretical knowledge. They must master fundamentals before moving on. They need to acquire a broad range of knowledge and be diversified. They need to be able to collaborate, communicate, and identify real world experiences. This will never be accomplished through cheating.

College representatives are very confused because on paper a student may appear diversified and knowledgeable. However, in the final analysis, a high school student that has spent most of their time cheating on homework can be completely lost when it comes to academia on a college campus. The foundation needed to build upon is nonexistent and if the student runs out of creative methods of sharing information, that student will struggle. Some students become discouraged and return home, others have to work twice as hard and become extremely anxious in this process. Either way, previous actions directly impact future endeavors. It is easier to justify being a bad test-taker as opposed to lackadaisical. Making excuses for absence of active engagement only fuels this vicious cycle.

Consequently, most colleges look at assessments as a means of determining the potential a student has for academic success. When a student has good grades, high test scores, and doesn't know any of the material it becomes baffling. Sadly, this can also be due to unethical practices that can occur in schools. For one thing, a high percentage of an educator's evaluation weighs on how students perform on tests, so educators have become experts on how to manipulate data whereof it appears as though students have a strong knowledge base even if they do not. A good question to consider is whether a national assessment is a true indicator of a student's intellectual ability.

The number one complaint from educators is "we teach to the test" Accordingly, teachers are pressured to force feed students the information they need to know to score high marks on tests despite actual learning taking place. As a consequence of this, students do not know how to study, prepare for tests, take notes, or become critical thinkers; which essentially are the tools that will lead to success later in life.

On the whole, what can be done about this cheating epidemic? Let's put this in perspective:

1. Kids cheat because they feel like they don't have a choice.
2. Teachers don't review work because they don't have the time.

Essentially, kids need to see the value in what they do and they are only going to see that if the teacher takes the time to check the work, explain it, and allow an opportunity for questions. This can be accomplished by assigning less homework, only instructing half the period, and allowing the other half for students to collaborate collectively or review the work, and inquire about the assignment.

With this in mind students working collaboratively isn't the same as cheating. Normally, cheating goes something like this:

"Send me math and I will send you French"
"Anyone have the bio homework- I have soccer tonight and no time to do it."
"Can you send me the history homework?"

Rather, when students work jointly together, they are using intellectual thought to make sense of assignments. By doing so, they are engaged and when students are engaged, they learn. A math class where a student is given 30 problems to complete and no one checks or reviews it to see if the problems are being done correctly essentially is meaningless. With this in mind, when students have to show their work the internet plays a significant role. Especially since a student can "Google anything" and when in doubt, "just ask Suri."

In turn, a transformation needs to occur from legislation. There is no doubt these legislators are baffled by the debacle happening in education today. In any case, policymakers may be unwilling to admit it is the guidelines they set forth that have wreaked havoc in education. By and large, pride needs to be put aside and in the final analysis a plan needs to be put into place that helps American students become better equipped to handle life.

Meanwhile, students need to help themselves and parents need to help their student. There are strategies that can be implemented that in the long run can aid students in becoming wiser, self-efficient, and accomplished. When students possess such power they are truly happy.

Doubly important young adults need to become more self-efficient. Today's youths are accustomed to doing little to nothing for themselves and as a result rely on everyone else to tell them what they should be doing. Similarly, the majority of questions I receive regarding college applications the student has not even attempted to read the information thus wanting me to complete it for them. Initiative is definitely lacking in this younger generation.

Contrary to what is easiest, perusing the application first and then asking specific questions is what is best. Students are never going to learn anything if everyone keeps doing everything for them. Even though reading the information and trying to understand how to respond takes longer, the process of thinking is essential to humanity ergo making sense of the world in which one lives.

Implementing Change

All things considered, for students to reach a level of feeling accomplished the cheating needs to stop. Helping students identify that taking these kinds of shortcuts can have severe implications is extremely important to their sense of self. On the other side of the proverbial coin, students that feel miserable about cheating may refuse to come to school. This is why a sense of optimism coupled with empowering students to be leaders in their own learning is of paramount importance.

Historically, mastery of skill is needed to acquire success in any given area. For example, take a person starting a new job at a restaurant, that person is first taught about the establishment, then the menu, the prices, and at some point how to help prepare meals. Many employees begin bussing tables or are a hostess before moving up to the next level. This gives a worker time to become familiar with the functioning of the restaurant. The employer does not have the new employee learn everything all at once because that would be a debacle whereby grasping one aspect is necessary before going on to the next.

Learning things simultaneously becomes confusing. For that reason, educational practices need to change. Students are being taught numerous concepts concurrently which cause ideas to get scrambled and misunderstood hence contributing to feeling overwhelmed or frustrated and in particular shutting down. Rather, taking the time to complete assignments, paying attention to underlying theories, and allowing time to ask questions when unsure of outcomes is a more promising approach. The burden to do well in school combined with high admission standards to colleges has accelerated dishonest practices through which students notice other students cheating and getting away with it so they do it too, basically to stay competitive. Nevertheless, information retained is minimal, core beliefs are comprised, and false impressions prevail.

Consequently, this generation has horrific speaking abilities, which is another flaw in the educational system. A communication class is not a graduation requirement in most districts, yet should be. Young adults not only fear public speaking and giving presentations but conversations in general. This is a looming concern because most jobs or careers involve some form of dialogue.

Parents have not become good role models in this area either. Many parents email, text, or post on social media when face-to-face conversations should be taking place. I am astonished how many neighbors and friends will talk to me virtually, yet when they see me, little is ever said. I think the comment "everyone is so busy" is just an excuse for people being "socially awkward." Discomfort seems to be disabling many people from accomplishing simple tasks. Students frequently report they are "uncomfortable talking to their teacher" so they avoid asking pertinent questions. Avoidance only exasperates the uneasy feelings they have making it more difficult to advocate on their own behalf.

Sometimes students do have the courage to ask questions and become deflated because they do ask a question because they do not understand the answer given and fear asking again. A student worries if they inquire further the teacher will accuse them of not listening. Often, when I have gone to a teacher on behalf of a student the comment is, "really, he never asks me any questions." Or, if I point out a student didn't understand the response given, perplexed the teacher says "oh, I wish they would have told me that."

For reasons such as this students need to start speaking up. Do not have parent's email the teacher, or counselor, students need to talk to these professionals themselves. Taking charge of one's own learning is the best way to promote maturity and growth. If the teacher comments to "look online" or "check your notes," then voice your inquiry more aggressively and state, "I already did and now I need help." Do not back down, true wisdom is derived from the process of gaining knowledge not just receiving the answers. When students just receive answers and forgo the undertaking of critical thinking application of intellectual thought becomes absent.

Parents can help by not inquiring on their child's behalf. Too often I get an email from a parent asking about something and the parent states, "he would have asked you himself but he is too afraid" or "he doesn't have time to see you." Even worse is when the parent sends an email to a teacher or coach and signs their child's name. Such action is not increasing the child's depth of knowledge. Children need to find answers on their own so they can gain confidence and are capable of decision making.

When a child knows a parent will come to their defense no matter what, they are encouraged to be untruthful, circumvent hard work, and disregard deadlines. They start to believe grades and test scores define them rather than ethical actions. Even worse, when parents continuously speak on kids behalf kids are not practicing how to build relationships and this impedes upon their success. They will never get practice at communicating if someone else is always doing it for them. Children asking questions might be uncomfortable but certainly manageable and most importantly, beneficial. Furthermore, they will acquire piece of mind knowing the answer; which in my opinion is invaluable because you can't put a price on piece of mind.

This generation of students lacks the ability to think for themselves thereupon always wanting someone else to tell them what they should be doing. Moreover, today's youth need to find methods of processing and recalling information to lessen self-doubt. There are traditional methods like note cards, outlining, or highlighting, but sometimes, those are not enough. If there is a lot of material to remember, or a not so interesting subject, then a more involved process may be necessary.

This could entail voice recording notes and playing it back, teaching the material to someone else to determine how well the information is known, or reading and rereading the information again for clarity. Somehow in education there is a misconception that students either know the material or not, they shouldn't have to review or practice it. That simply is not true. Practicing it is the only way a student is going to truly become better.

Relate this to a sport. Players practice with the team and the coach then instructs them to practice on their own. Some athletes will and some won't. The ones that do tend to perform better during a game. Life is no different. Students that prepare for tests on their own, tend to score higher marks. Every student I have talked to that has scored well on a test did so because of reviewing the material prior to a test.

Another study method that has proven to be effective is collaboratively going through material with others. For example, if students have a quiz coming up in history, a group can get together and review notes, ask each other questions, and explore the material together. Not only is this more pleasurable than studying alone, it can also be more insightful. One of the reasons studying with others can be so effective is often there are strategies for recalling material or pertinent information that perhaps a person on their own may not have thought of.

The trick with this form of collective learning is someone needs to be the leader and organize it. Most people don't want to take the initiative to plan a study group, but may be willing to attend one. This procedure also works well in the college setting. This is known as a small community of learners working together to reach a common goal. Some students have never experienced the results of hard work and expect to receive accolades per se for doing nothing.

Occasionally there are students that feel comfortable with the knowledge base they have yet the looming fear of not performing well can still exist. To help manage this type of anxiety students should consider meditating before taking an exam. Breathing techniques can help a person relax and focus. Concentrating on inhaling in and out can clear a person's mind and once the mind is clear, attention can be applied elsewhere. Meditation has been known to reduce stress, increase attention, and process information with greater clarity. By connecting with the unconscious mind, people have been known to rejuvenate and become inspired. A person can have tremendous benefits by cultivating meditation into their daily lives.

Student Capital

Along with meditation for healthy living a person should be involved in daily exercise and good eating habits. I realize this is nothing new, but you would be surprised how many people do not engage in this practice and schools no longer encourage it. In many school settings, kids are confined to the building all day long and not afforded the opportunity to walk around or go outside. School officials worry if given such liberties, students might get into trouble. On the whole students are getting into trouble anyway because they are restless and need a break.

Without a doubt increase in teen stress is subsequent to not being allowed to leave school for lunch anymore, parents chauffeuring kids everywhere, and less involvement in physical activity. Exercise not only relieves stress, but releases serotonin in the brain for feelings of happiness. When a person's serotonin level is down, the brain can transmit negative moods. These undesirable attitudes lead to feelings of anxiety, panic, and depression. Now imagine feeling that way and going into a classroom to take a test. A student is doomed before they even begin.

Dr. Krolczyk

Food also impacts a person's overall sense of wellbeing. When eating well, good feelings are present; when a person feels good more is accomplished. Numerous studies for various methods of weight loss have been performed, all with a different method of how to reach the same goal. Some strategies for losing weight describe counting calories, others mention reducing carbs or sodium. Conversely, there are approaches that suggest cutting sugar while other plans entail taking certain supplements.

In essence, losing weight has become just as complicated as everything else. Regardless, a person needs protein and energy to perform their best. Before a sporting event, many athletes have protein shakes, protein bars, cheese sticks, etc., because such items are known to increase energy levels. Therefore, a person should want their energy level to be at an optimum when testing and consider engaging in the same behaviors. If certain foods fuel a person's vitality then those foods should be consumed more often in general, but especially before an exam.

Another great tip for test-taking preparation is to put electronics away when studying. This strategy lessens the opportunity of encountering distractions and if the use of the internet is necessary a computer may be a more viable option. By and large continuous alerts from twitter, Instagram, face book, snap chat, and everything else preoccupy one's attention disrupting focus. In short, multi-tasking doesn't work. For this reason trying to accomplish studying and connecting to the virtual world at the same time has been unsuccessful.

Social media has caused so much interference in people's lives they are completely distracted and missing out on valuable opportunities. Fatality rates related to social media and driving have increased, family conversations have decreased, and kids have become more self-absorbed and disillusioned. There exists a lack of connection between the cyber world and real world and it has become a nuisance. People seem to have less interest in living life and have become more engrossed in what other people are posting. Such obsessions are overruling ambitions. The fixation of what others are constantly doing has become an unhealthy addictive habit.

In summary, below is a review of measures students can take to enhance test-taking abilities to achieve greater results:

1. Stop cheating.
2. Have the courage and confidence to ask questions.
3. Find methods to process and recall information.
4. Study with others.
5. Meditate.
6. Eat healthy and exercise.
7. Put away your phone.

Retesting & Open Book Testing can be Detrimental to Learning

Since at times there is a discrepancy between the grades a student receives and performance on tests, schools have been accused of not teaching kids what they need to know to be proficient on tests. An exam demonstrates fundamental learning and if students don't fare well then someone needs to be held accountable for the lack of knowledge students possess. The question becomes who? The blame usually is not placed upon the kids that perhaps cheat on homework, the parents that pay taxes to educate their child, or the system that cut funds in schools and increased staff responsibilities; therefore the only group left to blame is teachers. This is precisely what is happening in education today.

Sadly, a teacher's entire job resides on those test scores. To put this in perspective teachers have encountered multiple cuts in their pay, have higher premiums on insurance, an increase in workload and are threatened daily with the prospect of job loss. No wonder teacher educator programs are not inundated with students; who would want this type of profession?

More than likely, the next American catastrophe will be a shortage of talented educators. The levels of education teachers and college professors have and the lack of respect and pay is disheartening. Furthermore, most educators are truly dedicated to the profession. Consequently, it will just be a matter of time before all the nonsense of top-down management gets to them.

Plus, it is very difficult to support a family on a teacher's salary. Most educators have to supplement their income with another job; which takes them away from family and can become quite tiring and stressful.

Another sad realization with the infrastructure of education is teachers and principals have, like students, resorted to extreme measures to continue to meet local and federal mandates. By circumventing the system, they are dodging the problem and finding a way to placate the community and legislators that hold funding hostage. It is almost by default this is occurring because no one knows what else to do.

If teachers have high test scores, principals appear successful, and if the principals have schools with higher ranks, then the district gets positive feedback from its constituents. The local news brags about great performing schools and money is allocated to keep this momentum going. Life is good for all, until the child that didn't really learn the material goes to college. Instructors quickly become puzzled because a student that has high marks and high scores is not performing well. This must be a reflection of the college and its professors, so the blame game, finger pointing, and making life easier for the student, so success can continue with little effort, begins.

Peace and harmony is once again restored, until the student becomes a college graduate and has to uphold a job. It is at this point that some students come to the realization they need to step it up and although it may be a struggle, they need to actually learn how to complete tasks. Since there are students that can't cope with this pressure and don't know how to handle being accountable for themselves, they may withdraw from society all together possibly entering a deep state of depression. Others might become aggressively angry at the failed system and lash out on innocent members of the community. Neither scenario is good for a person's sense of well-being or for society.

I am not exactly sure what everybody thought was going to happen by making everything easier for the kids? I theorize the mentality was if the curriculum was more rigorous, kids would have to work harder. The same convoluted thought process continues to exist as elective choices are constantly being be cut and replaced with core subjects and advanced programs. This approach is damaging because actual learning is non-existent and then a mental health plan quickly accompanies it.

In comparison, a company that is struggling financially may cut workers and not replace them. Therefore, other employees are given additional functions. At first glance it appears as though this company is able to still succeed, but the inability of workers to keep up with more duties causes additional strain. So, some workers may cut corners and not thoroughly complete a chore or others will stay late and become bitter about it, while some go home in the evening and continue to keep working. In the final analysis employees are unhappy, less dedicated, and unpleasant towards fellow workers, patrons, family and friends. Gradually, less attention and detail is given to performance thus causing the company that appeared successful to crumble.

Here's another analogy; going to the gym for an hour is not the same as working out for an hour. Having a gym membership and belonging to a gym does not yield the same results as working out. Having a harder curriculum is not the same as making kids work harder. When you work out you are more likely to be in shape. When students pay attention, compete work, and study they are more likely to learn and be prepared for post high school. For a person's body to transform as a result of working out it takes time, dedication, and endurance. For a person to grasp the concept of new knowledge it takes patience, commitment, and hard work. These accomplishments are not acquired overnight. Rushing the process yields negative results.

Similarly, what appears to be happening in the schools jeopardizes student learning whereas student achievement is being rushed and results are not accurate. An example of this is the test and retest theory. Students have been afforded multiple opportunities to take a test over and over again until the score is acceptable. By continually retesting, students are not increasing their skills; they are just becoming more familiar with the material and test format hence responding differently to the questions.

In any event, a student is less likely to study if they know they can keep taking a test over. This format is justified in the teachers mind because students are given opportunities to do well. No doubt when students "perform well," the teacher is viewed as effective. Coincidently, some administrators encourage this process.

My 6th grader recently came home and informed me she had an essay question from a test that the teacher instructed the students to go home and "research it" and the following day they will answer it in class. When I asked her what the question was, she innocently responded "I don't know, it is written down so I didn't need to memorize it." When I asked her if she needed help "researching" the answer, she said, "No, we are allowed to bring in any notes we have, I will just print notes from google" I asked "then how are you leaning anything?" and she exclaimed, "I don't know, but the older kids get to use their notes on tests too."

Astonished, I asked my two high school students and sure enough this statement was true. I questioned teachers about this and was informed that there is too much material to get through so the only way to do it fairly is to let the students use their notes. One teacher stated that most days there is not enough time to answer student questions and with so many increased duties little time is even available to correct papers in which case students are missing valuable feedback. In essence, students have little direction on information being presented to them yet they are still responsible to know the information. I find this entire process uneventful.

I reflect on my own learning and how I tend to get confused or need reassurance that I understand the material correctly. My comfort comes from questions being answered. If this process is not allowed, then I would be going through the motions without retaining the information. Letting me use notes does not help me process the details or think critically. I am not being challenged intellectually to conceptualize or apply information.

This process lacking meaningful instruction is especially concerning because students are becoming conditioned to passive thinking whereby self-guided and self-directed thought process is diminishing. Moreover, students just accept information at face value and do not look beyond the surface. As a result they have become mindless, unimaginative, and limited in the complexity of finding solutions and resort to what is accessible and convenient. When college admissions representatives inform me students want the representative to tell them how to answer personal essay questions or what to write, it helps one understand that cognition of mental agility and integral thought process is lacking since harassing profundity has become non-existent in school systems.

Not surprising, instead of schools being an institution to prepare students for future endeavors, they have become cheating sites that eventually damage or harm a student's ego and self-worth. Even more devastating is how nonchalant students are about this cheating epidemic; they have even started doing it openly and freely. In any event, some parents and teachers know and turn their head the other way because they are not ready to face this tragedy.

Adolescents live in the here and now and don't comprehend how these dishonest actions may impact them later in life, so they are completely unconcerned.

Student Capital

When students are given answers but don't understand the problem, there is no conceptual thinking, analysis, purpose, or learning taking place. Education is changing at such a rapid pace and substantial information needed is being missed. Shifts in educational practices need to occur at a slower pace utilizing proper resources effectively to reach students' skillful assessment and reconstruction of information; otherwise students are being set up for lose-lose situations.

Cheating is almost like a bad habit that has become too difficult to break. Everyone knows the current process is harmful, yet continues to engage in it. The end result is a nation in crisis and lack of investment in Student Capital. By not investing in students and their needs this nation is in disarray.

Generally, when a student comes down and tells me he did poorly on a test, I ask what part he got wrong. Often, the student doesn't know. I find this perplexing because a student needs to know what they did wrong so they can correct it. Coincidently, many schools use common assessments and because of this, students are not able to review a test after it has been taken.

Teachers fear students copying the test and passing it along. Well, students have found other creative means of cheating, so for the student that truly wants to improve his learning, this mindset is not helpful. Students need the opportunity to review, discuss, and ask questions so they can understand the concepts and not continue to make the same errors.

Continuous improvement involves constant learning which entails a progression of understanding through trial and error. Even putting answers on the board after the test or talking about the questions/answers could be helpful. Many teachers expressed not having enough time, but that needs to change. Since student learning should be the priority, time needs to be allocated for after exam reviews. A student moving on and not knowing what was done incorrectly, yet are expected to improve, is backwards thinking. If a student has not mastered the first skill, they will never acquire the subsequent one. If working a job, they would be fired. In school, they fail.

College Board Monopolizing the Market

The College Board is a national organization developed in the 1900's asserting to effectively help students prepare for college. Services are provided promising to aid students in college readiness. The institution is not-for-profit but charges a significant fee to schools and to students for being part of the College Entrance Exam Board (CEEB) and for all testing materials.

Thousands of colleges use the outcomes of test scores when selecting applicants. There are 3 main tests offered; SAT, PSAT, and AP. Below each one is outlined in more detail. College Board dominates the market in U.S. testing hence allowing the non-profit company to charge enormous fees. Other issues include test security breaches, a complex website, an overload of information, lack of test preparation information, and extreme stress on students.

Dr. Krolczyk

SAT

The Scholastic Aptitude Test (SAT) offered by the College Board is a national test that measures college readiness and is considered a predictor of future academic success. This test is highly regarded by colleges. Some students may have a low Grade Point Average (GPA), but score high on the SAT, which indicates capability of learning. Other students have a high GPA, but score low on the test, which can be concerning to admission representatives. The subject matter on the test is said to reflect what students should be learning in school.

The main topics are critical reading, writing, and math with science and social studies being integrated into the various sections; which is known as cross-testing. On the SAT, there is no penalty for wrong answers, so it is in students' best interest to guess if unsure. Each of the 3 main subgroups (reading, writing, and math) is worth 800 for a total score of 2400. An average score is 1500; above 1800 is considered great and below 1260 could impact college admittance.

This is another reason why when students cheat on homework in school, they are doing themselves a major disservice not learning what they need to know to be prepared for this college entrance exam. A test like the SAT measures individual potential. The higher a student scores on this test, the more opportunities they have for scholarships. However students are not always aware of this.

Students also do not realize what they learn in class could better position them to score well on the SAT. Like everything else, schools rush through this process. Something as important as an assessment to determine a student's college potential should be given more attention by the high schools. Usually it is a school counselor that is the coordinator of this test and this is an additional duty to all the other duties school counselors have.

PSAT

Many schools offer the PSAT, which is a practice SAT test and is considered an indication of how the student may perform on the SAT. This practice test also helps students identify areas where they may need to apply themselves more or recognize a strength they can build upon since an overall score is given. When the PSAT is taken in 10th grade, schools use it as an indicator of AP potential; meaning AP classes the student might do well in.

However, this can be misleading because the results might list numerous classes, but the rigor and challenge still require hard work and dedication which some students have a difficult time with. Balancing college level classes (AP) with high school classes, sports, a job, and other extra-curricular activities can quickly become overwhelming. Students need to first be shown how to properly review the PSAT results, and then make a decision based on what they are able to balance.

Sometimes the index score of the PSAT taken in 10th grade is used to encourage students to take the test again in 11th grade. If the PSAT is taken in 11th grade and the student gets a qualifying score, they may be considered a National Merit Semifinalist, which means they scored one of the best in the nation and can compete to be a finalist. Even if a student does not become a finalist, just being a semifinalist is an impressive academic achievement which improves a person's odds of getting into competitive colleges and increases scholarship opportunities. The qualifying score to be considered a national merit semifinalist varies from year to year depending on the pool of students taking the test that year and how they score; the top 1% are named national merit semifinalist meaning they scored higher than 99% of peers on a national level. The metrics used to determine this is called the *selection index.*

The way the *selection index* is calculated begins with a weighing of the readiness of the 3 sections of the PSAT: reading, writing and math, which range from 6-36, adds those up and multiply x 2. That score is then compared with an index range for each state. This can also be determined by looking at sub scores: which range from 120-720. To determine the index score, drop the zero at the end of the overall combined sub score for reading and writing, multiply by 2, then add the math score with the zero dropped. For example, if a person scored 530 on reading and writing, dropping the zero would make that score 53, multiplying this by 2 would equal 106. If that persons score on the math is 560, drop the zero so the score reflects 56; add 56 for math to 106 for reading and writing the total index score reflects 162. Is this confusing? It most definitely is. Was it meant to be? An educated guess tells me yes.

The state determines the cut-off score based on the pool of juniors scores. The average score for National Merit Scholarship Competition (NMSC) in the past has ranged from 209-222. Keep in mind; the cutoff score varies from state-to-state, and year-to-year. A commended student is one that scores high, but not high enough to continue in the competition. The school is notified by the state and then informs the student if they meet the criteria for one of these statuses.

Often schools will encourage students that took the PSAT in 10th grade to take it again in 11th grade with the notion the student may qualify as a merit semifinalist. The more students that qualify as a national merit semifinalist, the more impressive the school looks. Schools glamorize the scholarships available if students receive a qualifying score, but neglect to inform people that only 1% of the nation is in this range and millions of students take this test.

If a student scored in the 140 range, chances of getting between an index score in the range of 209-222 are slim and since students are so over-tested to begin with, one less test to worry about may be better. Since parents aren't aware of all the facts, they might place pressure on their child. When the student doesn't get a high enough score, the student feels like they let everyone down, when in actuality, they were not even close to becoming a semifinalist.

To avoid being misled, questions should be asked like "what is the qualifying score for our state?" "How many students last year were semifinalists?" "How close does the student have to be to even have a chance?" Some schools send notices to parent suggesting their child take the PSAT in 11th grade, based on how the student scored in 10th grade. However, the bar set to qualify a student to receive a letter is low, which once again misrepresents information causing unnecessary anguish.

Dr. Krolczyk

The PSAT results offer a plethora of information so students can better prepare for the SAT. The problem is, no one explains this to students or parents and test results go underutilized. Since test scores are so significant for college admissions and scholarships, schools should host a parent night, hire a testing coordinator, or permit time for counselors to explain the various ways results can be used so students see the value in it.

Even having students peruse this tool during class time would prove beneficial. It should be done more than once too, because like everything else the more they become familiar with the advantage of this information, the more likely they will be to use it independently. This is one way smaller caseloads for counselors, specifically to build stronger relationships with students, can allow these conversations can take place will prove extremely beneficial to a student's academic future.

What is important to know about the PSAT score report is the student is given an access code, listed on the front of their PSAT results, and that allows for personalized feedback, practice tests, college planning and career exploration. On the back of the test, are the overall results and the answer the student selected, and if wrong, the correct answer is listed. Students are given back their testing booklets and should take the time to review this. Students and parents can visit College Board for more information regarding this test and Khan Academy (online), which has an exclusive partnership with College Board and offers free comprehensive practice material.

However, multiple students have reported when retaking the SAT and using Khan Academy as a prep tool scores have gone down. Students are then directed to study material that can be purchased. One can't help but wonder if this is deliberate so the non-profit organization can increase profits. There are general strategies that can help a student prepare for the SAT/PSAT which include data preparation and analysis (logging and keeping track of data), understanding words in various contexts (words can have more than one meaning) and evidence based answers (derived from reading). Students should do whatever they can to sharpen those skills.

AP

An Advanced Placement (AP) exam is a test student's pay money for and if a qualifying score is achieved, they can be given college credit for the course which would then exempt them from taking that subject in college. The intent of the AP course is to prepare students for the exam that correlates with the course. The AP exam is a national test and usually two weeks in May are allocated for these exams whereas everyone in the nation takes the same test on the same day at the same time. During those two weeks, a specific subject test is given in the morning and another one is given in the afternoon.

Students must sign up for these exams through their school and must take the exam on the designated day it is offered (there are a few exceptions that apply for a late exam; students would need to see a school coordinator for more information if a circumstance prevents them from taking the exam when offered). The goal is to have every student in the nation taking the exact same test at the exact same time. This way when scores are compared, no one had an advantage to the test. When a late test is given, it is a different exam and still constitutes a designated day and time for that subject test. This way all late exams for a particular topic are given the same day across the nation.

What is considered a qualifying score for colleges to accept credit varies from college to college and students should seek this information out prior to taking an AP exam. Students should also reflect on the overall scores of the school for a particular subject matter. The score ranges from 1-5; 5 being the highest. A score of 4 or 5 is usually accepted by a university for credit, scores of 3 vary by colleges, and credit is usually not granted for scores of 1's or 2's. A school that tends to have more qualifying scores perhaps does a better job preparing students for the exam.

National overall scores should be looked at so a student has an estimate of how difficult an exam can be. If a student has certain colleges in mind they would like to attend, they should engage in further inquiry to determine which exams and score ranges unforeseen danger can occur. The institution has the right to determine which subject test credit can be granted for credit so it is important to note not all colleges accept all subjects; regardless of the score.

Unfortunately, students have become like a flock of sheep and educators are the one's herding the flock. Like sheep, students have become accustomed to just following the direction they are given. By doing so, they have trusted that they are being kept safe. However, if the shepherd is unfamiliar with the grasslands, unforeseen danger can lure.

When educators are unacquainted with requirements, unanticipated disappoint can occur. Criteria for college's change at rapid rates, so the student needs to step up and keep themselves informed. Just like some sheep have a natural instinct to become more familiar with their surroundings so they can lead a flock home during tough circumstances, some students have taken the time to explore college standards so they can be successful at college. When a sheep gets separated from a herd, that sheep becomes tense because they do not know where to graze. When a student gets detached from the information they need, they become agitated because they do not know what to do. If more students would take the time to browse college standards themselves, they would be less frantic about the process.

Schools are not invested in the outcome of AP scores and it is the outcome that benefits students. For the most part, getting students to take AP courses is top priority. With that being said, students that perhaps are not prepared for the rigor of an AP course are being encouraged to take one and if they take the test and acquire a low score, they feel unintelligent and disillusioned.

First of all, many students have gotten into the bad habit of "calling in sick" the day of an exam for a class. By doing so, they are privy to the exam format and answers from other students whom have already taken the test for any given course. Upon return, the student takes the test in the hall where no one is able to oversee it and usually scores well, thus offering the impression they knew the information.

Since students are not afforded this same scenario when taking an AP exam; scores tend to be low. The disconnect is a student can be getting an "A" in an AP course, but only score a "1" on the AP exam; which points to the student not really knowing the material. A school invested in Student Capital has a screening process for AP courses, helps students build on their strengths, and properly prepares them so they are confident when taking the exam. Student Capital is devoted to outcome and the process in which desired outcome is achieved.

Teaching Students to Conduct Research

We live in an era where students have an abundance of technology at their fingertips. At any given time, they can pull out a smartphone or tablet and look something up. This does not mean they know how to conduct research, utilize different search engines, compose and interpret a comparative analysis or understand data. Nor do most students comprehend there are other search engines for scholarly articles other than Google.

In particular, most students may not understand what a scholarly article is or how to properly site one. Paraphrasing and plagiarism have skyrocketed due to this lack of knowledge. Additionally, at the college level students have a difficult time distinguishing between quoting and paraphrasing and do very little critical thinking. Even more concerning is when a paper that has been plagiarized is pointed out to a student; a nonchalant demeanor tends to exist. Many students are under the mindset copying work from the internet is no big deal because this is what they have been conditioned to believe is acceptable. Students, especially in high school, have the attitude, "I will worry about how to that later." However, knowing some of this information sooner will benefit them later and they simply do not realize that.

One of the reasons for students inability to properly conduct research is students are on technology overload. By this I mean there is too much information and it has become overwhelming. Take applying to college for example, students have found what was once known as a simple process (you apply, get accepted, and go) to be arduous and confusing. College representatives come into the schools and students don't have a clue what questions to ask.

Students need to learn how to decipher what is significant and what is not. The representatives are simply advertising for the college they work for hence offering a very appealing sales pitch. In short, students' not knowing enough about a given college or the college process contributes to students shutting down when they get to college. What they were told and believed to be true about a particular college is not always the same once they get there. Above all students can be naïve and gullible and have difficulty when trust has been broken. Students also have a hard time accepting that they made a mistake by not verifying the sales pitches they have been given.

With this in mind, a person would never buy a car, electronic device, or piece of furniture without researching it and considering several factors. Yet, when it comes to educational endeavors, decisions appear to be quick and hasty. The difference is when a person overspends on a household or personal item; they may experience buyer's remorse or are inconvenienced and take the item back. Contrastingly, if a poor educational decision is made, students are accustomed to everyone else to fixing it thus releasing them of any burden. This is because public schools fear school of choice and virtual competition, so they give in to student wants rather than focusing on their needs.

By not sticking to high standards, holding on to core values, or building relationships schools are not acting in the best interest of students. Consequently, this eventually causes demise in student learning and when students don't learn it further validates in a parent's mind choosing an alternative form of education. School systems need to do a better job explaining the purpose in whatever process is being used to prepare kids for post high school so students are interested in being an active part of that process. This will alleviate a lot of confusion and self-doubt once a student gets to the next level.

It is also important that people do not just take what they are told at face value. Doing so can be crippling. A lot of organizations are profiting on sensitive topics. One event I attended offered training for schools on how to effectively address suicide prevention and promised to offer best practice strategies. The solution was to train teachers to identify and address students with suicidal tendencies.

A teacher that has overcrowded classes, curriculum driven lessons, and high level stress having to demonstrate student growth is now given one more thing to do. Despite suicide being the second leading cause of death in the United States, this preposterous method is supposed to be considered an effective strategy. It is incredibly disappointing leaders did not think to question what informed this technique as "best strategy." Mental health experts exist in the building and are not being utilized to the best of their ability which is why there is a generation of anxious and depressed students.

A survey was conducted with high school seniors on what they needed more information on and the results were as follows:

Careers	32%
Colleges	43%
Scholarships	58%
Financial Aid	34%
Social/emotional	04%

Student Capital

Skill Trade	01%
Tutoring	01%
Study Skills	13%
Nothing	18%

Looking at these results, it is clear to see where students place the most value and that is on attending and paying for college. This may be because society as a whole has placed so much emphasis in these areas. Schools in general have created an injustice to kids by focusing so much attention on academic performance and rigor and downplaying skilled trades, the process of learning, and emotional intelligence. The areas students indicated they did not need more information are not due to having a strong knowledge base of these topics, rather these are capacities students do not deem essential for success. If they did have a knowledge base of these areas, the catastrophic state education currently is in wouldn't exist.

Until there is a paradigm shift that takes place in the schools, research for the sake of learning needs to start in the home and students need to take it upon themselves to be balanced, well-rounded individuals.

Schools have become a model of business thriving on devious advertising. The pendulum has swung from what is in the best interest of student learning to pass the student through the system to boost marketing techniques and continue receiving state funding.

Parents need to be aware that what they are being told from school professionals is not always what their child needs to get to where they have to go. It is easy to entrust professionals, but remember; they too exist among the broken system and often are expressing "the company line." Therefore, educating oneself through personal research is paramount to future endeavors. Students need to keep in mind no one is going to look out for them to the extent they can look out for themselves, so they need to take the time to do it.

As an educator with a multitude of experience and education, I am exasperated with everyone identifying the problem but unwilling to be part of the solution. When the argument is presented that kids come to college unprepared and lacking substantial knowledge for success I want to bellow "what did you think would happen?" Educational funding has been cut and mismanaged so much that it has become impossible to offer quality learning.

In a desperate attempt to continue functioning, like students, educationalists have figured out how to elude the system so it appears as though knowledge is being transferred and shared, but really information is doled out in such mass quantities it not being processed. Furthermore, kids simply are not coming to school and no one is taking accountability for this. This is not working smarter with less time and less money, it is instead imprudent and injurious to kids and society as a whole.

When initiatives of this type first took place, I would hear of students getting into college, but not finishing because of the discrepancy of what they knew and what they needed to know. Now, students are not even able to sustain jobs because so much more is lacking besides intelligence. A lot of kids miss school with open-ended doctor's notes and teachers are asked to exempt work, modify assignments, and adjust tests so this student that was barely present in class can pass. Where is the accountability? When did schools become so fearful they kowtow to parental demands or give in to medical notes lacking specific dates or details? Doctors used to work with schools and parents to develop plans that appropriately and ethically addressed student needs; now, many medical professionals thrive on affluence and greedily treat clients that are not ill or provide prescriptions that are not medically necessary. As long as this behavior continues, so too will the dysfunction in the educational culture.

School officials seem to spend the majority of their time now servicing the high percentage of students pathologically diagnosed with ailments that have been reported to be directly impacting their learning. As a result of this, little time is left for the average student that is putting forth his/her best effort, but may still have questions or concerns. As unfortunate as this is, it has become a reality that no one wants to admit is happening.

The best thing a student can do is become equipped with research skills to find the information necessary for personal success. This includes knowing about transferability. What that means is students should be familiar with college level classes taken in high school through AP or at a community college and if those classes will be accepted at another institution of learning. It becomes shocking to students to find out classes taken at one place may not transfer to another.

If students start at a community college they should make sure courses selected are universal so if they continue on and attend a university they will not have to take as many classes towards their degree choice. There are many transfer websites students can use to figure this out. The problem is students don't realize this and end up taking courses that do not transfer which becomes discouraging.

The same concept is becoming a growing concern with students that go to charter or virtual schools. The curriculum may not be the same as a public school, so if credits are not accepted when transferring to a public school, it could delay graduating from high school. Another problem with for profit entities is students sometimes have not engaged or participated in learning, yet still received glorified marks, then become fundamentally behind.

This becomes convoluted because when actual learning takes place, the student is at a loss. If a student received overvalued grades at a private institution and then transfers to a public entity that student may struggle academically and this can lead to a complete meltdown. Since the student was successful previously, the public school is blamed and pressure is placed upon teachers to do what the private school did; pass the student through. Usually if that student does manage to graduate from high school, they may end up taking developmental classes to learn the basics for a college curriculum; which is what they should have been learning in the high school setting, but did not.

Shockingly, when a declaration is made of a gap between k-12 and higher education everyone is in awe. What society does not realize is the gap is much deeper than anyone could have imagined because the process to properly educate today's youth does not exist. The appearance that education is taking place has become a farce used for the purposes of ranking higher on social media sites.

To rile the issue further, students are reporting poor counseling and guidance at the college level and as a result of this, some students end up in a career path that does not lead to job opportunity. Or in some instances, students are told they need to complete the master's program to acquire employment in their chosen field; which equates to more time and money. This is information they were not aware of prior to embarking upon their educational journey because no one told them, they didn't ask, and didn't look into it.

College level students need to ask about job growth, networking, and career prospects to better ensure they are not headed down a dead end road. If someone is not available to inquire, students need to research it on their own. Being curious enough to want to know an answer is the smartest way to ensure future stability. A student's entire path may be altered due to information gathered; and that's ok.

How does a nation of students with copious amounts of information at their fingertips stop cheating and start seeing the value in their learning? How did a country that prospered with innovation more than any other place on this earth get to a point where mental health issues, terrorism, and crime have guided our way of life? Instead of seeking the "American Dream" people are in pursuit of safety, living daily in fear.

This is never what anyone wanted for themselves, their children, or their grandchildren, yet what America has become. How can creativity, safety, and self-worth be restored so happiness, instead of terror, prevails? Respect, gratitude, and genuine empathy need to overpower contempt, greed, and apathy. People need to not only start honoring thy neighbor, but to also love thyself. When a person becomes their own worst enemy; danger looms for others.

CHAPTER 5
THE CURRICULUM DEBATE

"Every child has the ability to learn, but not every child has the desire"

~Dr. Krolczyk

High School Course Offerings are Dreadful

My son and I were having lunch one day and he asked, "Why don't they teach kids how to write a resume or apply for jobs." I replied, "I thought they did." He commented, "Not in any of the classes I have had." Sitting across from me was a teenage boy taking college calculus, physics, government, English, college psychology, and a college seminar class. It was at that moment I realized schools really don't teach kids the skills they need to transition to the real world.

I was curious now, so I further inquired, "why don't you just look it up on Goggle, isn't that what your generation does?" He chuckled and said, "Mom, Google might show you a resume, but it doesn't explain how to do one. It is like looking up a job, the internet might tell you about the job, but it doesn't teach you how to do it." Now I understood the needing-acting concept even better. Kids need the knowledge of how to complete a task, not just the information on the task. Schools can act on this by demonstrating how to do something because academic intelligence is not the only trait that is employable. Students need so much more that is not being offered or taught.

Every district website I peruse I notice a technology plan; I have yet to find a post high school plan. School Boards need to follow state guidelines, but can also incorporate other meaningful curriculum, like a job shadow class. This could entail a one or two hour block, junior year, which instructs today's youth on:

1. Building a resume, applying for jobs, work ethics, mock interviews, how to dress for an interview/job, speaking skills, and the implications social media can have on employment.

2. The second part of the year, teens can learn how to find a job, and actually work at one. This is a great opportunity to find out what their likes and dislikes are. Instead of taking an interest inventory, they become actively involved in a career field. Schools can network with local business to have students do internships/job shadows.

A lot of schools may assert they already do this by having a school co-op program. Consequently, not many students are even aware a program of this nature exists and often, when a student does become aware they are unable to fit it in their schedule due to rigorous graduation requirements. Even worse, the students that are in a co-op program are not benefitting from it. Furthermore, there are stipulations to be involved in co-op such as GPA, attendance, and discipline.

I had a student that wanted to be involved in the co-op program and go into the skilled trades; which this particular student would have been great at. Unfortunately, this student had been suspended for ten days of school for having a Juul on him (tobacco product) and due to this suspension did not qualify for co-op. Having such a strenuous curriculum with no relief caused him to lose interest altogether and stop coming to school.

For this reason, a mandatory career prep class can benefit all students, not the elect few that are involved in co-op programs. Basically, with the current model for a work related experience students just leave school early and go to work. They also have to have a "related" class in their schedule, so potentially this program would not be an option if they are unable to fit this into their schedule. They are not taught anything about employment, work ethic, resume writing, and skills required for particular jobs.

Similar to school, they are going through the motions and after a while it becomes mundane and meaningless. A class that helps students to understand the value of employable traits would be more significant and are attributes students would benefit from for the rest of their life. A school employing student capital would institute a course with these benchmarks because it is what students and society need.

Junior year would be the best time to implement this type of course because after exploring various interests, learning types, and personality styles, another class could follow senior year that incorporates looking up colleges and college degree programs, career growth, how to compare and contrast features of institutions, degrees, certifications, and trades. Students can research what steps are involved in applying for college or certifications, what role standardized tests play, how to apply for FAFSA, how to apply for local and federal scholarships, how to send a transcript/test scores. Essentially, this 2-part course would entail how to become a better student while allowing time to complete information necessary for post high school success.

Rather than invest in people that can make connections with kids, school systems invest funding in software that students don't' understand or care about. Forcing students to utilize these software programs is no different than forcing students to par-take in curriculum they struggle with. The more a student struggles, the less interested they are. Spending less money on technology and more on staff to guide and direct students is what this generation needs. At what point does the United States Educational System realize people, not electronic devices, is what makes school systems great.

High school students do not know, nor have the time to complete necessary research for post high school endeavors; hence the increase in anxiety. I viewed a student's agenda that quite honestly was stressful to even look at. The student suggested she could not even enjoy homecoming because the entire night she was thinking about all the things she had to do, including review college program offerings, admittance requirements, and seek scholarships. It made me very sad to think that education has become so stressful whereas a beautiful young lady is not able to relax and find pleasure in a pinnacle event. As much as she is told to relax and have fun, she boldly states, "I just can't; I am constantly worried about being able to fit everything I need to do in a days' time."

You know how you don't really pay attention to something until someone points it out; so I started to ask around and found many students are vexed with the same or similar concerns. As a result, students question how to better manage their time so as to complete all the tasks they are assigned and once they stumble upon the realization it is literally impossible; they completely shut down.

Often, the parent completes the application process for their student because of how busy and stressed the student is. Subsequently, the student is not involved thus causing greater confusion. As previously stated, if career and college guidance was offered as a class, students would have the time to complete the necessary tasks involved in this arduous process, be afforded the ability to ask questions, and gain a sound knowledge base when making critical decisions post high school. A course of this nature would alleviate a whole lot of angst.

The benefits of incorporating a class like this into a school day are enormous. When restructuring education, the area of career guidance needs to be looked at closely. If a student is going to succeed at what they do, they need to be stimulated. The best way to elicit enthusiasm is by active engagement. If a school is going to offer career guidance than the person in charge of it needs to be afforded the time to actually complete this task; in other words, this should be the main focus not an additional responsibility. The multi-tasking era is a huge failure, so schools need to shift away from it and incorporate single tasks that can be done accurately and completely. The mistakes being made from lack of attention to detail have become quite costly.

Student Capital is about investing in kids and their needs. One way to accomplish this is by investing in one's staff. When I observe staff being more miserable than the students, there is an obvious issue. In fact, part of the reason the curriculum being so awful is a problem is even teachers are no longer passionate about their work. Arguably, when passion is not present listening, learning, and interpreting is difficult. By the same token, forcing kids to learn causes them to reject it.

Be what it may, if learning was appealing, kids would want to put forth the effort to gain the knowledge regarding the information being presented to them. With the current educational system students see no value gained in the information being presented to them so they do not care if they retain it. For this reason, today's youth need to:

1. Find what they are good at and build on those strengths.
2. Try different things to discover inner passions.
3. Manage emotions, like discomfort or anxiety, to work for, rather than against them.
4. Make connections and form relationships.
5. Understand their purpose in life.

These 5 things can help a person embrace challenges. Anxious feelings should be used to inspire and motivate so a young adult feels more accomplished and less like a loser.

I had a conversation with a dad the other day where a student no longer wanted to come to school. The student was basically bored, not interested, and anxious. Medication for anxiety and depression did nothing for him, the reason medication did nothing for him is because he didn't have a medical condition, he had a bad case of, "I hate school," which is a feeling or emotion, not a disability. All the same, it was hurtful to the parents.

So we took a look to see what was causing this student to dislike school so much. The student was a 10th grader and in his schedule he had: Algebra 1, English 10, French 1, Biology, U.S. History, and Web Page Design. Sounds like a great schedule right? What about the 11th grader that has English 11, Economics, Chemistry, Health and Wellness, Algebra II and German I? When Parents email me and state their child "wakes up every morning in extreme pain or vomiting, has lost weight, cannot eat, is severely depressed and wants to drop out of school, " I get it, I totally get it.

Most of these students have anywhere between 35 and 50 absences and are failing all their classes. So I ask, what is so great about these schedules? These classes are hard, homework is given in each one of them, the subject matter is not of great interest, and students feel like complete failures. Asking kids to do one or two things they do not want to do may be ok, but asking them to sit all day long through classes that have absolutely no appeal to them is a bit much. In turn, this lack of investment in kids is causing major stress hence implicating their health.

Michigan State University released a study indicating anxiety has increased by 16% and depression by 25% over the last few years; calling this an "all-time high" (State News, 2016). Action taken to address these concerns included adding more staff to the student health services. The study mentioned meeting the changing needs of students. Mobile technology was even created to supplement in-person counseling. This study is a prime example of not focusing on student capital whereby the stimulus's causing increased apprehension is never addressed. Until it is, strategies put into place will prove ineffective.

Anxious feelings are a trickling effect most often starting at the high school or middle school level. To further exasperate matters, a counselor's main role in secondary education is about the ability to fill out paperwork than the capacity to guide students and this appears to be a direct correlation to increased student despair. Furthermore, mobile application can never replace a live person and society needs to stop thinking that it can. What you really hope for every child is a successful life. What constitutes a successful life is waking up every day and wanting to go to school or work or coming home and wanting to be there. To state the obvious, this is not occurring.

Determination, resilience, and preservation come from doing things that matter. When a curriculum is impossible to complete, youths find ways around it. They do so by lying, cheating, and faking answers. They know this is wrong so they feel guilty. Not only do they feel bad, they become paranoid constantly looking over their shoulder to see if they are going to get caught. This is like the adult that lies on his taxes to get extra money, or engages in dishonest conduct for profit or gain, then is completely stressed about it. Wouldn't it be so much simpler to just do things right.

While the gain of doing things the right way can take longer and not show much profit until later, it is still worth the effort. Learning is similar to this whereas students may not see the gain in what they are doing at the time they are doing it, but in the long run may benefit tremendously by knowledge garnered. However, by not offering any sense of reprieve, students are discouraged altogether. Offer students a reason to come to school and they will. It is alarming how many students report "I don't think I have ever been so stressed over school in my life."

One of the reasons kids cheat so much is because the classes they are forced to take are difficult and uninteresting. Somewhere in the country a group of politicians got together and decided if kids took classes that were harder, they would be smarter. Now this nation is facing an educational crisis which clearly proves this theory wrong. Yet even though everyone knows this practice doesn't work, no one has done anything to change it.

Rather, leaders tiptoe around the matter in hopes that it will disappear. When a major crisis occurs, mental illness is chiefly stated as the culprit shifting focus from the damaged system. Meanwhile, an individual is left feeling dysfunctional when by and large it is the system that is broken, not the individual that committed the act. This is evidenced by similar tragedies, repeatedly occurring.

Dr. Krolczyk

I recently sat in a meeting with a student, his parents, and several educators and this student had an entire schedule of "required" courses and had basically "shut down." In the meeting, everyone was trying to figure out why the student wasn't doing his work and he flatly stated what should have been obvious to everyone in the room, "I am just not interested, school is boring and I get way too much homework, it is impossible to keep up."

This is a student that had a passion for photography, was interested in business, and would be great at debate. However, as his guidance counselor, I was unable to put any of those classes in his schedule due to mandated curriculum. He, nor I, had any control over which classes he took. Additionally, he was a special education student whom struggled academically, emotionally, and now socially because he is so frustrated he doesn't feel like doing anything. A student that could have flourished has now given up. This is one of many examples of why this nation is in an educational and mental health crisis.

Kids need and should have options because when they are forced to do things they do not want to, day in and day out, it becomes superficial and the only reason they do it is to check it off a list. Finding the easiest way to check it off becomes their mission. If a student is not working, they are not learning. When a student is doing something they have absolutely no interest in, they are not working. The only way to get better at anything is by doing it. Students are not going to put forth the effort all day long to do something they don't like.

Pupils find school to be exhausting, depressing, and extremely stressful. Telling kids something has a purpose is not convincing enough. Doing less can lead to more given the fact that kids then won't shut down and accomplish something as opposed to nothing. A statistic perhaps overlooked is the amount of kids "getting high" before school "just to make it through the day." In reality the nation has a bigger problem than projected. These kids have become the majority, not the minority. When pressure increases, so too does the illegal substance thereupon leading to an increase in overdoses.

I am not convinced school systems are investing in kids when everyone within the culture of a school is miserable. Recently I went to a restaurant for Mother's

Day. The wait staffs were amazing. They were friendly, accommodating, and pleasant. The food was good, but the service was great. A lot of restaurants have good food, but not all restaurants have great service and that made the experience enjoyable for my family.

When people have enjoyable experiences, they return to the environment that provided it. Comparably in education students constantly complain about how crabby, unhappy, and irritated teachers have become. Regrettably this makes students dread the high school experience therefore not wanting to return to that environment no doubt increasing school refusal rates. The assault on teachers needs to stop because essentially it directly impacts kids. I view this scenario no different than parents in a household that continuously fight, it affects the kids too.

Parents can help their child by not buying into the mindset that just because a schedule is more rigorous it is better. If your child does not want to take a third year of a foreign language or an advanced placement class, don't make them. Have your child instead select a class that appeals to him/her. Parents have been brainwashed into thinking if their child does not take the highest level of classes offered, then they are behind. When parents tell me this, I often ask "behind what?"

Regarding the foreign language, not all colleges require two years of a language. That is not to say taking a foreign language wouldn't be helpful to a student for a perspective career, but if a student is not ready or even interested in the subject, forcing them to take it could result in apathetic behavior and diminutive effort. Students will learn a language when they are ready for it. The same theory holds true for advanced courses. These courses only benefit a student if the student is interested in the topic and puts forth the necessary effort to achieve desired results.

Students need to stop rushing and should take the time to think things through before making decisions on classes. A student that is good in math may want to try accelerated math, but when coupled with other accelerated, honors, or advanced courses the workload can become too much eventually compromising the students ability to excel in math. At the same time, if a student has a job or is involved in extracurricular activities, that student may not be able to dedicate the time to an accelerated curriculum. Students need to consider numerous factors before signing up for subjects that involve extra time and dedication.

A student should actually run through what is thought to be a typical day with the selections he/she intends to make. The reality is an intense schedule can be quite overwhelming. By trying to visualize the workload and how time would be managed, a student would be able to determine realistically if finding balance is possible. If completing everything does not seem feasible, a student should reconsider other choices of classes than an accelerated curriculum. Opportunities will always exist and a student does not need to engage in all of them at once.

All things considered, kids need individual personal guidance on class scheduling. Students need help exploring various areas that may be of interest to them. Counselor caseloads should be 150-1, so the counselor has an opportunity to meet with every student, discuss credits, student interests, classes, scholarships, college opportunities, skill trades, and transfer equivalencies.

Too many students are missing pertinent communication related to these important topics.

When students are guided properly, they are able to make more informed decisions. I cannot begin to emphasize how many times a student has come down trying to get out of a class because they signed up not knowing what it entailed. Sure, part of it is the students fault for not inquiring, but part of it is also the breakdown in communication. Do students even know where to find the descriptions of the classes? Who tells them? How often is it updated?

This is where government officials that assert kids can do things quicker and better with advanced technology are confused; they can't, they aren't, and no one shows them how. Just because millennials know how to manipulate social media does not mean they know how to utilize every piece of software or every website available. This misconception has become detrimental to student success.

With that being said, parents can better direct their child by taking the time to discuss with their child what the course descriptions entail, what may or may not ignite their child's interest, and what their child still needs to meet graduation requirements. Some courses can be used to replace others and it is important to understand which ones would meet this criteria. Students are given scheduling information and afforded little time to review the material before it is turned back in. Taking more time to review the scheduling literature and inquiring about things is extremely important.

Too often students sign up for a class, don't like it, want to change it, and are unable to. It is much better to take the initiative to understand what a course is about before taking it. This will also help avoid pitfalls of kids struggling. Accountability needs to be placed back on the student and that includes taking proper measures to assess what truly is best for their individual learning. It is critical that students read the course descriptions for classes and understand what is involved and if a student is unsure where to find this information, they need to ask.

If a student wishes to pursue an advanced curriculum they should know what is involved in obtaining one. I continuously hear from students, "this class is overwhelming, it is stressing me out, I have never taken an advanced class so I did not know what to expect. I am a very busy person and don't have time for hours of homework." Strangely enough, the scenario is always the same.

The student usually comes down crying, followed up by a parent phone call, then a doctor's note for severe anxiety. This entire dilemma could have been avoided if the student did some research ahead of time and knew what to expect. Another student may have mentioned "the class is easy," but simple for one may be complex for another. Perhaps that other student has more time, or isn't taking other advanced courses, has fewer distractions, or knows how to study.

A student's reason for taking a particular course needs to be individualized and only that student can decide what would be best for him/her. I fear kids taking classes because they have been told it looks good on a transcript, not because they desire to learn the information. Furthermore, if they do not take an advanced class it does not mean they are not a collegiate candidate. The mindset of AP being a predictor of student success has to change because it is causing too much of an emotional upset for kids.

The educational system needs to recognize elective classes are a significant part of student learning. Optional courses offer students a break from required courses and contribute to relieving stress; which students desperately need. For example, many schools do not offer orchestra anymore, so something a student could have cultivated and found solace in is no longer an option. Classical music is a form of art rooted in traditions and soon such traditions will no longer exist. The current music kids listen to does not appear as enriching, soothing, or inspiring like symphonies and bands from the past.

Kids need to appreciate long standing customs of music. Kids also need to recognize long standing traditions of art, manufacturing, design, carpentry, mythology, and philosophy. These courses are all electives that used to be offered in schools, but have become overruled by advanced, honors, and accelerated classes. I believe there is a direct correlation between student's inaccessibility to choose classes of interest and higher levels of anxiety and depression. Students need to take back control of their lives and not allow this to happen.

Similarly, it does not matter how much information educators make available, at the end of the day it is the student's responsibility to do something with the information that was provided. The mindset that if a child fails everyone else needs to fix it is not allowing the child to develop, learn, and grow so he can later prosper in a diverse global society. Part of protecting a child is helping them make choices and not offering false pretenses. Parents do what a student should and could do for himself, I often hear "I know I shouldn't help him, but I don't want it to jeopardize his future."

In reality, there are consequences for certain acts of behavior and if students are continuously protected from facing these consequences they are not prepared for when their shelter no longer exists. Even though some penalties are more severe than others, when a student is led to believe no penalties at all exist they experience greater confusion later in life.

Helping a child and doing for a child are different concepts; one can help by not doing it for them and allow them the sense of accomplishment when they figure it out. It is almost cruel to take that away. Young adults will eventually figure things out, or learn how and whom to ask for guidance, some adolescents may take longer than others to develop this skill, but eventually all youths will get there if given a purpose. When a person lacks purpose they become disconnected and a disconnected person becomes destructive.

A hungry person learns how to cook. A really hungry person learns how to hunt. Feeling the pangs of hunger will motivate a person to gather and prepare a meal. When that person sleeps, they will acquire more energy and as a result will seek food in larger quantities presumably being better prepared to eat when hungry again. In comparison, being well-fed absent of the process of seeking and preparing a meal may permit a person to sleep well but when they awaken they are in search of a purpose. If no purpose can be found, out of boredom they go back to sleep. This time however, that person has no desire to awaken because they feel like a purpose does not exist.

Student Incongruence

School systems are notorious for investing in technology but in my opinion never considered that maybe a district is investing in the wrong technology for the wrong people. I was in a school and noted all the secretaries, bookkeepers, and counselor printers were archaic. When the secretary, whom was extremely busy apologized for how long it was taking for her out-of-date printer to print I glanced in the principal's office and noticed not one state of the art computer, but two.

Not wanting to bother him, I smiled and waved and then noticed while the secretary was backed up with students and parents the principal was looking at real estate because he was selling his condo and buying a home. He mentioned how having the double screens made it so much easier to accomplish this. It is misleading to think that because a principal is the head of the school he is busier than others. Ironically, schools are filled with incongruence's.

For example, an automatic email gets sent from a data base to students with my email address on it reminding them about college visits. When a student stopped me in the hall and showed it to me I didn't know anything about it. The student bashfully commented, "I thought this email was from you and that you cared." I informed the student I cared very much and it was at this moment that I realized there is not as much value for kids in an automated system as there is with personal contact. Incidentally, people have become replaced by systems and that is a huge mistake when attempting to service such a vulnerable population like young adults.

Ultimately, the college visit the student showed me on his phone only 2 students attended. This made no sense to me because it was a college many students have inquired about. However, relying on mobile technology to facilitate a college visit for students is impersonal and as a result negatively impacted the turnout. Every time I turn around, there is a new application, device, software, URL, website, blog, twitter, or Facebook page offering kids creative solutions to their future and it quickly becomes confusing.

At this point, students are bewildered as to which source offers the direction they are seeking because there are too many sources to peruse and little time to dedicate to become familiar with any of them. Furthermore, many of these sites exaggerate the truth listing information that is self-reported by the company rather than a true reflection of the population. With this in mind when studies, such as the Michigan State University one, suggest implementations needing to be made to "meet the changing demands of society from students," what is not addressed is the cause of such demands (The State News, 2016). One direct cause is the lack of services provided for career education in secondary education and higher education. This disconnect has led to increased student demands.

In this case creating more mental health services, which is what many universities are doing, does not increase career awareness. All the literature in the world is not going to peak student interest; relationships with individual students and gaining their trust will. This is because in the long run students know people, not systems, have their best interest at heart. Doubly important, saying an organization cares about people is not convincing enough; showing it does by addressing the right factors is more evidenced based.

Dr. Krolczyk

One of the aspects students neglect to look at when prospecting a career is job growth, especially during rapidly changing times in a global community. As a result, many students graduate and are unable to secure employment. This is one of the reasons the Every Student Succeeds Act (ESSA) regardless of applying to a public or private school is a model for disaster.

This movement focuses on minorities and low socio-economic students. However, for a student to succeed school officials need to look beyond race and see a student's potential. On the other side of the proverbial coin, society is noticing an increase of Caucasian students not being accepted to universities due to the fact that an institution wants to keep its minority numbers up to look good and obtain that nice federal government money. To believe that the world is fair is to be naïve. No matter how hard the general public works to be fair and equal, there are inherent biases which, sadly, we all experience.

Civilization is quick to blame lack of success on disparity in ethnicity. This is because finger pointing is much easier than accepting a system has been created that is destructive to all. It has been estimated that one-third of students moving on to obtain a post-secondary education are properly prepared for the complexity of the university style of teaching (Moore et al., 2010). This lack of readiness is a perilous issue for universities as they are seeing an increase in the number of students failing due to a fundamental lack of knowledge.

This loss of knowledge is a direct result of students no longer getting the information taught to them in a manner that is meaningful. Instead, what they are being taught are answers to tests for rote memory recall, whereas the process of theoretical thinking is missing. More and more teachers are offering re-takes on exams thus allowing students to research the answers. This process is meaningless to the student becoming nothing more than an activity for completion rather than a basis for intellectual thought. Given this fact, standardized testing creates undue stress on the part of the student because they are not properly prepared.

What happens next is students feel so pressured to do well that when they do not do as well as they wanted to, they get depressed, start to feel hopeless and generally do not continue their scholarly ways (Moore et al., 2010). This continues into higher education where parents and the federal government are paying for classes that these students fail. This causes another area of frustration for the student when others start demanding an explanation for botched grades.

Restating the obvious, everyone learns by a different method so as a rule a student and an educator understanding the student's learning style is helpful when preparing for a test. Educators changing tactics of instruction to suit the students learning style can help to increase the students' knowledge base. Certainly to do this, educators must care about their students and have fewer students to care about. There has been a noticeable increase in the amount of teachers with uncaring attitudes (Moore et al., 2010). Educators must first care about their student's success, because student success means something was learned something from the teacher. At the same time, "lack of concern" can be a direct reflection of how poorly an employee is treated; almost to the point of abuse. When this occurs passion is crushed.

Despite the fact that high school is tightening its requirements for graduation, many students need remediation once they get to the university level (Cohen and Kisker, 2010). This is a sad realization because stakeholders like to think they are providing the best education for children, but sometimes many kids fall through the cracks. These students get less of a chance because it takes them longer to graduate, possibly causing them to get frustrated and stop going to school altogether.

The high school experience is more than just academics. There is a lot of maturing and growing that happens during those four years of high school. Likewise, some students mature more slowly than others and while they excel academically, they are unable to navigate the higher education world. Being similar in many ways, students fail to realize that being good at something requires study and practice, years of it.

Conversely, it is not realistic to expect success without hard work. Nonetheless, this is exactly what is occurring. What happens is when a student does have to put forth effort to achieve results they are used to getting with little to no effort, they become totally lost.

Presumably, the mental health industry is capitalizing on educational systematic errors. Some health facilities advertise "crippled by anxiety" or "brain balance" alluding to something being drastically wrong with the individual. Aside from an extremely flawed system, the individual is fine. It would be folly to think all of the problems in education are reflective of students' mental health capacity.

I will use the example of my son and his ACT score. Students traditionally take the ACT during their junior year. It has been hammered in the general public's minds that students need to take this test in 10th grade to see where they fall weak and what they should be working on. On average, most 10th graders do not fare well on this test and for this reason a heightened fear of not succeeding in life prevails. All things considered, students are not academically prepared to take this test in 10th grade and subsequently become discouraged.

Comparable, my son never took it in 10th grade, took it during his 11th grade year, then again towards the end of his senior year, in which case he scored a 30 out of 36. In conclusion, students are better prepared during later years of high school. Doubly important, was his self-esteem. Overall, he felt confident in his ability to succeed post high school. In Contrast, this feeling could have been easily damaged if pressure was placed upon him to take the ACT prematurely. Meanwhile, this is exactly what is occurring to students across the nation at epidemic levels. Their ego is so low they do not even want to try again.

With attention to self-esteem, students need to understand preparation and experience is relevant to success. I ran into a computer science professor and in conversation she mentioned her language barrier and having to take the English-Language Test (known as the TOEFL) 3 times when at college. In short, she had to overcome this obstacle before she could reach her goal. Overall, her grit led to her accomplishment.

She sustained that it was difficult, and at times she was unsure, but she knew if she persevered the end result would be worth it. By the same token, she had others encourage her along the way. Ultimately, it was this reassurance from others that boosted her spirit. Constant encouragement helps a person to believe that anything is possible; no matter how impossible one believes something to be. In the final analysis, instead of seeing a mental health expert for an incapacitating feeling of anxiety, she inspired others by flourishing; which is a much greater feeling.

A scenario such as this one involves relationships and connectivity, both of which require time. In order to afford time for interactions to take place professionals need less things to do, less people to do them with, and more flexibility. The more things a person has to do and the more people they have to do it with the less opportunity there is to be flexible. When students are connected they are productive. Since there exists a generation that lacks initiative, connections need to be encouraged and school professionals need to be able to have the support to do this.

This is so important because students need to understand how good it feels to accomplish something. People by nature become more accomplished when encouraged. As an educator, I am continually reminded of "close and critical reading," which refers to reading that is meant to be careful and purposeful with a direct focus. Well how about trying close and critical student investment which would entail intentional planning of working with pupils so they can acquire a greater sense of higher level thinking hence allowing them to feel accomplished. When a person feels accomplished, it makes them want to work harder to continue feeling prideful. On the contrary, when a person feels shameful they close themselves off and become isolated.

Confidence, more so than anxiety, contributes significantly to who we are. Yet, society has become overly indulged in decreasing people's exposure to atmospheres or situations which stimulate anxiety. The problem with this is by avoiding an anxiety causing situation a person never learns methods in which to desensitize them to the stimulus and conquer it. The inability to overcome an anxiety ridden situation leaves one with less confidence.

This was the premise of the Netflix T.V. series "13 Reasons Why." It is a fictional story about a high school girl that takes her own life and leaves 13 tapes to people as to their role in why she killed herself. In any event, these people are left feeling responsible for this young girl's death whereof she lacked communication skills and confidence. On the whole, blaming others was easier for her than taking responsibility for skills she needed, but didn't have. With this in mind, I offer 13 answers to 13 reasons why:

13 Answers to 13 reasons Why

1. People need to compliment others more.
2. When adults talk to kids, kids feel validated.
3. Students need someone they can trust and talk to.
4. Kids need to know they can talk to an adult without consequences or they won't talk.
5. When kids talk, it is important not to judge, the minute they feel judged they stop talking.
6. The school counselor is part of the system and it is the system that is flawed.
7. Hire more counselors where talking to kids is their main task; perhaps then this nation won't be in such crisis.

8. With so many kids unable to manage their anxiety it is difficult to assess who really is in danger and who isn't.
9. Blaming others for ones actions is weak.
10. In an era where personal communication is lacking, being kind to others is that much more important. You never really know what could be going on in another person's world.
11. It is much more desirable to build one's self-confidence than to stop every bully from bullying.
12. Harassment of a sexual nature should always be reported; a victim deserves to be heard.
13. There is physical health and mental health; both need to be taken care of.

Clearly one can see how emotions define actions. Allowing the availability of school professionals to help young adults sort through feelings, concerns, worries and questions can make a world of difference. School systems tend to be reactive instead of proactive. For example, a local high school had 7 suicides (actual suicides, not attempts) in one school year. It was then that this district decided to add more school counselors.

Advanced or Regular: Do Students Even Have a Choice?

It seems as though the nation has gone overboard on the value of taking an advanced placement (AP) course and as a result students are experiencing a great deal of torment. The United States has become a nation where folk's mistake advanced placement for academic success. When a college admissions advisor looks at a student's transcript, they look to make sure core classes were taken. Those core classes can be advanced, but don't have to be. In essence, what they are looking at is how well the student performed overall; which can be misleading.

Many parents confuse this national push to take advanced placement classes as absolutely necessary for college entrance, which simply is not true. This type of thinking can be very damaging because then the student receives additional pressure from parents to engage in advanced studies. If a student is not prepared for the precision of an advanced class, they should not be taking one. The reason they should not engage in a curriculum they are not prepared for is because they may struggle to keep up with the pace or cheat immensely which causes massive guilt leading to severe stress and sometimes depression. Hence the plaque of anxiety the country is currently experiencing among teens.

It may sound bizarre that an entire country is experiencing an increase in anxiety over course selections, but on the other hand it makes sense. Such an extreme outcome is due to pushing students to sign up for an accelerated curriculum. I see the daily stress this has caused teens, even to the point of where they no longer want to attend school, which is very sad. I find this disheartening because if students did not take advanced classes, they can still be successful, and may even be encouraged to pursue a career path rather than feeling depressed and worthless.

Students sign up for AP classes for different reasons. Students sometimes take an AP class because friends are taking the same course, parents and teachers encourage them to, or they elect a course that they have heard is easy and does not present much homework. However, if the AP class is not an area they are strong in or a subject they are interested in, they may have difficulty paying attention and keeping up with the material.

This can lead to excessive tension, restless sleep, and eventually total shut down. Educational leaders and parents being assertive in having kids take AP classes may seem smart, but isn't wise because kids get to the point of hating school. When this occurs, districts are following a bad model and a better one needs to be created or more students will be at risk for failure and depression.

Here's an example. I met a student that desired to be a radiation therapist. When exploring classes needed to succeed in this career multiple sciences came up. However, instead of taking an AP Chemistry or AP Biology course, the student signed up for AP European History. When I inquired as to why the response was one I have heard often. She flatly stated, "Currently in my honors Chemistry class I re-take all my exams to get a good grade; I heard AP European History is easy and does not have a lot of homework. All I want to do is raise my GPA."

The students end goal was having a higher GPA, not learning the material to succeed in her career interest. When I pointed out that a different class, even one not accelerated like physiology may be a better option for future endeavors, with a pained look she expressed, "That class would be too hard and may lower my GPA, currently I don't have to do anything and have a 4.02." Standing before me was a youth that has been taught the appearance of knowledge is more important than knowledge itself. The student has clearly bought into the concept of falsified learning and I fear the results when this student gets to college and the lack of knowledge possessed becomes exposed.

Teachers have expressed concern over the amount of pupils in these advanced classes caught cheating. It is as if more time and effort is put into trying to cheat than studying and doing the work. One teacher stated, "I have never in my 22 years of teaching caught so many students cheating in an accelerated course." The mere fact that students have excelled in the area of cheating is ghastly. Yet students have accepted this is what needs to be done in order to be successful.

Dr. Krolczyk

Some of the various methods students use to cheat is taking picture of tests, googling answers, group messaging, writing the letter answer for each question on a sheet of paper to give to others, as well as faking being ill to take the exam at a later date in a different place, putting cheat sheets in mechanical pencils, boots, sleeves, or waistband. The reason they cheat is because they have not completed any work, declare being uncomfortable asking the teacher for help when in reality embarrassment exists because they have not done any of the work, do not know how to handle getting a low grade, have done nothing to study or prepare, and are only concerned about the end result as opposed to the process. While cheating in school has always occurred, the increased pressure of difficult, uninteresting classes has resulted in increased cheating.

Pressure is placed on everyone else to fix the problem, ironically, without ever addressing the stimuli that caused it. I revert back to the curriculum mandates that led to this crisis, in addition to coddling students when they are anxious about these curriculum mandates.

At this point, this type of mindset reinforces this educational crisis.

When schools attempt to remove feelings of anxiety by making it easier to complete a difficult curriculum, without ever looking at changing the curriculum, the problem becomes cyclical. Until schools realize this method of treating the problem is unrealistic, the problem will continue to exist. This is because ultimately the dilemma remains within the students' inability to attain information seemingly necessary to be adept.

There exist various thoughts and arguments about the benefits and risks of participating in higher level courses. Each theory offers compelling views on why a student should or should not engage in a college level class while still in high school. At the end of the day, the decision needs to be individualized on what each student feels best meets his or her needs.

One belief is that if you take an AP class it can increase your GPA. This is somewhat true, but not entirely. The majority of schools give a boost in a grade if it is an AP class. This boost ranges from .5 to 1.0 of a higher percentage, so if a student got a "B" and the high school gives a .5 boost; it would be like getting a "B+." Where this negatively impacts a student is if a student got a "C" in an AP course , even though the school may give a .5 boost, this "C" reflects a "C+," and is still a lower point value than if the student took the regular course for that subject matter and received an "A."

By the same token, if the student did receive an "A" did they earn it with integrity? If the student cheated because the class was too difficult, the grade won't sustain them after high school because what they should have learned and didn't will become evident when practical understanding of the subject matter needs to be applied. This is the crisis and confusion colleges are seeing and one of the main reasons anxieties are perpetuated at the collegiate level.

As mentioned previously, parents and students have this misperceived notion that if they take an AP course, it "looks good," however looking good and being good are not the same concept. When a college looks at a transcript to determine acceptance and scholarship amount, the determining factors usually include GPA and test score. Ivy League schools tend to look more towards classes taken above and beyond the regular curriculum.

Most universities posit a regular high school program is rigorous whereby if a student does well in it, they should be prepared for the demand of college coursework. Students that augment learning are the students that will succeed, and by the same token, just being in an advanced program does not amplify learning. Students and parents need to remind themselves of this when teachers and administrators try to push kids into AP classes.

Of important note, College Board respectively claims to be a non-profit, national, organization that prepares students for standardized tests. The organization infamously advertises the ability to connect kids with more opportunities and college success. In any event, some claims made by this company tend to be misleading. This non-profit business is affiliated with so many for-profit industries that parents and kids can become confused on what is in their best interest.

For example, on the College Board website for fee waivers under the paying for college section, a person is directed to a site that offers financial aid information.

This is a service and costs money. Financial aid is free, so why would anyone need to pay for this service? They don't but might if they don't know any differently.

College Board also charges students to have test scores sent to colleges. It currently costs $15 for each college scores are sent to. One score can be sent for free if the student lists that college at the time they take an AP exam. The issue with this is many students do not know which schools they plan on applying to at the time they take the test. Furthermore, without knowing the outcome of the test, some students are hesitant to send scores. I find numerous free resources on the College Board website which lead to purchasing materials or services. It is most unfortunate that a non-profit organization nickels and dimes people for money.

One of the biggest issues with a radically designed institute like College Board is those that benefit the most are politicians. The premise of the organization is to have students sign up and pay for services with promises of getting better scores. Presumably, paying for services is not what the company claims, but nonetheless it is exactly what happens. Students are encouraged to sign up and pay money for academic seminars, study guides, prep materials and more to better prepare for an AP test.

The additional engagement in academics becomes exhausting and the cost can be very stressful. Likewise, this process is similar to grooming student athletes being that coaches mislead families into spending thousands of dollars on additional training and extra camps. Parents go along in hopes it will increase a student's chance of making a particular team, or increase opportunity for scholarships. Incidentally, if the majority of kids are engaged in these additional trainings, then none of the kids are standing out. Moreover, if a kid is not passionate about sports, forcing additional training will cause tension.

Likewise, if a student is not dedicated to taking an AP exam, being involved in extra preparation can trigger anxiety. As has been noted, forcing kids to do things becomes discouraging. Granted, they will do it on their own when they are ready and that is if they even do it at all. In other words, when something holds value to someone, they will be inspired to do more of it despite encouragement or discouragement from others. For this reason, decision making needs to be individualized in view of maturity level rather than aptitude. The heightened anxiety that is being provoked with youths, based on how they perform on these AP exams while still experiencing the coming- of- age, is disgraceful.

By and large College Board is intrusive with the information they collect for marketing purposes. Take the PSAT for example, which is said to be a practice SAT exam, but school systems use it to identify/push kids into AP courses because it also is said to identify AP potential. Aside from the basic information like name, address, and phone number, which should be more than enough to identify a student, it also asks about what courses the student is taking or plans on taking, if they can send the student information on scholarships and colleges, ethnicity, language, religion, college major, grade point average, and parents highest level of education.

Other than basic information, the rest of the questions are not necessary for test-taking. In any case, students do not realize this marketing ploy and check yes for literature to be sent. As a result, an excessive amount of literature gets dispatched to the home hence becoming overwhelming. The advertisements are not filtered to meet individual needs; rather it is mostly ads soliciting different services or college programs.

Incidentally, the AP answer sheet takes it a step further asking for the students email address. Some students claim to have deleted their email accounts because of the vast advertising filling their inbox. No doubt College Board will argue these sections are optional, meanwhile students are not advised of this. For this reason, young adults fill in those unnecessary sections thinking it is what is expected of them. Regrettably, this process backfires given that the overabundance of promoting post high school products or service's suppresses youths.

Consequently, a student develops dismal attitudes about post—high school and such wretched feelings are viewed by others as not caring. Ironically, the pattern developed is unknowingly a consequence of a student doing what they thought was best. Even I as a parent become annoyed with all the solicitation my kids get from colleges and started just throwing them away. Flyers, post cards, and letters that are misrepresentative, deceiving, and very confusing to me as an adult; so you can understand why I wouldn't want my child to read any of it. As I have said, investing in students properly and not through deception can alter this unpleasant worry that is causing teenagers so much grief.

Sadly, people get caught up in what they are being told rather than the truth. A perfect example of this is schools that participate in Equal Opportunity Schools (EOS) whereas the goal is to increase the amount of minorities or students on free and reduced lunch taking AP courses. This is supposed to be done by having a conversation with identified students and determining what is preventing them from taking advanced courses and helping them to make a decision in their best interest. However, that is not always how this task is carried out.

Since EOS requires data to be entered about these conversations, some school officials are held accountable if this task is not completed. So what happens instead is students are told, coerced, and in some instances threatened to take AP classes. When student X was caught skipping, he was told by an administrator, "I will not suspend you if you take an AP class next year." This particular student happens to be on free lunch. The student is not strong academically and felt trapped. Moreover, this is not how the program is supposed to be carried out. Not surprisingly, this student now has a bad impression of advanced classes, feels overwhelmed, and is less invested in his education.

In 2011, College Board started giving awards for districts that increased the amount of students that took AP courses and also scored a 3 or better on an AP exam. AP scores range from 1 to 5, 1 being the lowest. Some states had districts which originally qualified for this honor but decreased significantly in following years in student AP participation, like Arizona, California, Florida, Illinois, and Michigan. Other States had quite an increase in the amount of students taking AP courses, like Massachusetts, New Jersey, Pennsylvania, Tennessee, Washington, and Wisconsin. Some states over the years stayed the same, like New Hampshire, Ohio, Oregon, and Texas.

More than likely, some states took the approach of encouraging kids that should be encouraged while other states gambled by pressuring all kids. It would be interesting to note the suicide rates of teenagers in these states and if there is a correlation between the methodology of assessments and depression. Legislation continually overlooks the possibility that a connection could exist between a student's sense of hopelessness subsequent to that same student feeling dejected from a low score on these exams.

Some educators theorize that even if the student does not get a passing score on an AP exam or a high mark in the course, being in an AP class and hearing the information on a more challenging level better prepares a student for college. This may be the case for some students, but certainly not for all. Learning is individualized and just being present in a class does not mean a student is engaged in listening. In fact, many students shut down and experience high levels of stress or find ways to circumvent the system by copying another student's work. The high levels of stress sometimes become so unbearable students shut down and stop coming to school.

Student Capital

Equally important is the mere fact that the process of cheating defeats the purpose of taking an AP course since there is no contribution to muscle memory, which is repetition of doing something so it comes naturally. This can be why some students have a good grade in the course, but a low test score. In these types of situations students have not connected value to learning and generally speaking may not relate current actions as contributing factors to future endeavors. Until the educational system changes and student capital becomes a priority this problem will continue to exist.

By and large there exists debate on grade inflation with AP courses. Ironically, most teachers believe there should be a screening process for students taking an AP class. Presumably, the selection criteria should involve academic ability as well as academic motivation, regardless of economic status or cultural diversity. Given these points, many higher educational institutions are suspicious of the marks kids receive; especially since recently grades have not been a true indication of student capability.

Dr. Krolczyk

On the whole, when a college admissions advisor receives a student's transcript, it appears as though the student is performing well; but not all students are putting forth the necessary efforts to accurately reflect the marks they earn. Interestingly, this concern first surfaced in 2006 yet has been ignored since (Pope, 2006). The grade system is meant to offer an overall judgment of the capability of the student, by way of contrast this is no longer the case. That is, letter grades have turned students into pieces of data and nothing more. Individual accomplishments of students are no longer celebrated therefore causing students to feel miserable.

Presently speaking, many students go to college with unrealistic expectations. Students of this generation think classes will not be difficult and upon realization that college is meant to be challenging are unable to cope and quickly flunk out. Sadly, this desire to be spoon fed causes laziness in students and thus a vicious cycle of neediness perpetuates itself. Some students may not be suited to move on to higher education, at least not without some help. Parental guidance tends to be lacking in this process. While students are inexperienced and do not perhaps know any better, it is dreadful parents allow this type of neediness to exist. In my opinion, these parents may have been raised with the same mentality they are instituting.

When speaking to college admission representatives from Michigan and Ohio and asking what difference it made on a student's transcript if they took AP Classes, most responded that if the student got a qualifying score on the exam (which varies for each college) potentially a student could receive college credit. Many colleges consider a 4 or 5 a passing score and some colleges accept a 3(although recently many colleges have raised this score to qualify for college credit). Colleges admissions advisers do look at courses taken, but have indicated a core curriculum is rigorous enough and if a student wants to challenge themselves with advanced classes, it will benefit the student in the long run, if they actually learned the content. Some colleges even preferred that students did not take AP courses because the class may not have been taught at the higher level it should be and if pertinent information is not retained by the student this will impact them when proceeding to the next level.

With all things considered, how can students decide if taking an AP class is best for them? This can be a difficult decision to make. Students need to keep in mind that an AP class should be college level work; therefore they ought to expect to dedicate a lot of time to homework. When students take multiple AP courses at the same time, they may have difficulty keeping up with the workload, especially if they are also involved in extracurricular activities and/or have a job.

I always tell students if you are in a regular class and are bored or feel you need more of a challenge, try an AP class. The students I have found to be most successful with the advanced curriculums start with one class, and then gradually increase over the years. The students that jump full force into them tend to experience higher levels of anxiety and stress. Students truly interested in exploring their potential in an AP class should take the time to read the course description and make sure they understand expectations. This way a student can make an informed decision. One of the worst mistakes a student can make is to take multiple AP courses and not do well in those classes hence bringing down their GPA.

The Change in Curriculum Through the Years

Applying to college is fun, exciting, and an indication of a new adventure. High school seniors anticipate this next phase with exhilaration. Students gleefully visit colleges with parents or friends and come back elated about future aspirations. That was 28 years ago.

Presently speaking, students dread the college application process, fear this next phase, are overwhelmed to a point of mental disability, and have little ambition. One of the biggest differences between now and then is the curriculum, being that by the time a student gets to the college application process they are completely burnt out, overwhelmed, and stressed beyond belief. Another huge difference is the emphasis schools place on grades. Additionally, the loss of connectivity and intimacy between the student and the teacher has resulted in less direct feedback, ultimately impacting student learning.

In 1989, a student needed 22 credits to graduate, of those 22 credits 11 were elective choices. The vast majority of schools were open campus, meaning students were able to leave for lunch. Students also had the capability of taking a skilled trade course for 2 periods, could graduate early or were able to leave school grounds early as long as graduation requirements were being met. Since less graduation mandates existed this was an easy feat to accomplish. Furthermore, academic subjects were non-specific and for this reason students had options and flexibility.

The average ACT score in 1989 was 18 and doubly important the typical amount of AP courses offered were 6. Above all, music and art were highlighted on school profiles to entice enrollment. During this era the leading causes of death among adolescents were heart disease, cancer, stroke, and unintentional injury.

On the other side of spectrum, in 2017 students still require 22 credits to graduate, but the colossal difference is of those 22 credits, 17 are core credits leaving only 5 overall elective credits, during a four year span. In fact, this doesn't even include the Ethics requirement projected for 2018. Moreover most schools are closed campuses and students are not permitted to graduate early. Academic subjects are delineated, in which case students have less flexibility and options.

The average ACT score is 23 and most schools offer between 25-30 AP courses. The majority of school profiles emphasize AP exam scores and state testing exam scores. Meanwhile, the leading cause of deaths among adolescents is unintentional injury, suicide, homicide, and illness. Where suicide was not even a leading cause in 1989, it is one of the major causes in 2017. The academic pressure students are facing could be what is contributing to an increase in teen suicides.

Since test scores have increased, one might conclude that offering more AP classes has led to an overall increase in test scores. However, one could also theorize that more AP offerings have led to an increase in adolescent deaths. The additional pressures placed on adolescents presumably have caused an increase in anxiety. On the whole, high levels of anxiety have been

linked to depression. Generally speaking, when people are depressed suicidal thoughts are present.
Since society places so much emphasis on grades, numerous students have resorted to **CHEATING**.

Knowing this is immoral, some students experience extreme guilt which exasperates an anxious state of mind. Meanwhile, other students are totally accepting of the cheating phenomenon because they realize it is the best way to survive a broken system. To further complicate matters, some teachers tend to encourage this behavior by offering multiple chances to re-do exams or tests. There is even one credit recovery/enhancement program that allows a student to re-take a test 5 times and with 5 multiple choice answers the student is bound to get 100%. When this grade is then placed on a high school transcript, it is deceiving of the knowledge base acquired. Furthermore, some students then have an advantage over other students because of accessibility to this method of recovery/enhancement.

Graduation requirements in 1989

English 4

Math 2

Science 2

Social Studies 2

Physical Ed. 1

Electives 11

TOTAL=22

Graduation Requirement 2017

English 4

Math 4

Science 3

Social Studies 3

Foreign Language 2

Physical Ed. .5

Health .5

Online learning Experience

Electives 5

TOTAL=22

Dr. Krolczyk

Regarding the 17 core credits now required (this varies from state to state but is still significantly higher than from years back), students can apply for a Personal Curriculum (PC), Flex, Department Approved Career Technical Education (CTE), Testing Out, 21f, Dual Enrollment, Stem (science, technology, engineering, and math) or STEAM (science, technology, engineering, art, and math) pathways, or Early College Programs-all of which involve a counselors guidance and an abundance of paperwork for the counselor to fill out.

Essentially, fewer counselors exist in the school system and duties and responsibilities of high school counselors have drastically increased. As a result of the amplified workload little time is left to service students. Since students are not being serviced, many are unaware of options available to swap required credits. For this reason they follow the curriculum outlined by the state leading them to shut down and stop coming to school. One has to wonder if states have identified the need to "swap" credits; wouldn't it just be simpler to "change" required credits? This certainly would alleviate a whole lot of trauma.

I use the term "trauma" because that is exactly what is happening; students are traumatized by school. Never before have there existed so many kids seeing a psychologist, therapist, counselor, or medical professional who prescribes multitudes of medication just for a kid to function on a daily basis. Is there something wrong with the kids or is there something wrong with the system?

Emotional upsets are routine occurrences in and outside the school. School counselors are so busy with "paperwork" and "testing" no time is left for social emotional needs; social emotional needs have increased due to a fallen broken structure. Healing and change will never occur in a damaged system. Hurt, confusion, and self-doubt will continue to control outcomes.

In 2014, there were 1,354 suicides reported in Michigan (Michigan Department of Education, 2016), an increase of 39 percent since 2000. According to the Michigan Department of Education (2016), "Students are reporting significantly higher levels of anxiety, depression, and stress-related problems than they have in the past," and "Research indicates there is a current mental health epidemic affecting students and their school success."

It is important to recognize that in 2008, the MDE announced, "The only way to ensure that all high school students graduate ready to succeed in college and careers is to require the same high-quality college-preparatory curriculum for ALL students" and "To be successful in today's economy, ALL students will need education and training beyond the high school diploma." Essentially it was determined that all students needed to attend college without first understanding that not all students are college-bound.

Learning requires training overtime with lots of practice, and if students are cheating their way through high school they have not mastered skills necessary to acquire success in a higher learning institution. Furthermore, today's student is focused on what others want rather than what is in their heart. A closed heart is a diminishing heart. College requires time and effort and if students are not prepared for this type of commitment they will fail miserably. Better guidance at the high school and college is needed so fewer students fall prey to non-transferrable credits, huge amounts of debt, and degrees that are not recognized in industry.

These wounds will not be healed if better guidance is not offered. Negatively speaking, however, with the current state of affairs better guidance is an impossible feat. Markedly, the role of the school counselor should be post high school advising, career guidance, financial aid and scholarships, class selections, opportunities of skill trades, and sense of overall wellbeing. Yet, instead school counselors spend their time enrolling new students, interpreting transcripts, creating and documenting personal curriculums, explaining flex opportunities, discussing early college programs, enlightening students on dual enrollment options, offering AP advising, talking about credit recovery, reviewing summer school information, consulting on 21f online options, and monitoring student graduation tracks.

Schools counselors are also the AP, PSAT, SAT and State Testing coordinators. Furthermore, school counselors write letters of recommendations (which colleges weigh heavily on), assist with educational development plans, write 504-plans (which have increased exponentially due to more anxiety disorder diagnosis's), assist with homebound services, manage school refusal, refer to alternative learning, evaluate credits for graduation (which has become more complex with all the options), aid students with testing out, explain dual enrollment, support English Learners, help Special Education students, create and review accommodations for ADHD students, write behavior plans, manage conflict resolution, handle harassment issues, bullying issues, service and refer students abusing substances, have anger issues, need grief counseling, have self-esteem issues, are experiencing gender dysphoria, exhibit debilitating anxiety, display extreme depression, and perform suicidal assessments. School counselors are expected to perform all of the above mentioned tasks as well as respond to parent phone calls and parent and staff emails.

Everything has become more involved. For example, when a new student enrolls, it is no longer from another public school- it can be from a charter school, online school, from being home schooled or another country; in which a transcript and matching graduation requirements has become a more laborious task. States, such as Michigan, are struggling for resolutions and keep developing ineffective strategies.

- In 2001- Protect MI Child
- Also in 2001- U of M Depression Center
- In 2003-Coordinated School Health Program Model
- In 2004- Strategic Alternatives in Prevention Education
- In 2010- The Anti-Bullying Policy
- In 2011-The Social Emotional Learning
- In 2012-Adaptive PE More physical activity in school [how about allowing students to leave campus]
- In 2013-School Based Mental Health Partnerships
- In 2014-Restorative Justice
- In 2015-In-school suspensions
- In 2016- PBIS- positive behavioral intervention and support
- In 2017- OK 2 SAY

By students not being properly serviced at the high school level, schools are more likely to encounter poor school attendance and higher dropouts' rates. Additionally, students are more likely to experience emotional instability, lack problem-solving skills, inability to think critically, and have very low self-esteem. All of these factors work against the Every Student Succeed Act of 2015. Everyone is so busy trying to keep pace with everything the minds and bodies do not have an awareness of what is happening to souls and hearts.

Statistically speaking, after the Columbine shooting in 1999, counselors were in high demand and when more counselors were servicing students, suicide rates were down. In a desperate attempt for school districts to balance budgets to be fiscally responsible, counselors were cut. Just as bad, when other support staff got cut, counselors had to pick up their duties.

A solution to this was to bring in outside counseling services, which will never work. The reason this won't work is because students form a relationship with their counselor and that relationship is relevant in servicing the diverse needs of youths. Counselors have intentional conversations with students based on that student as an individual. Everyone is so quick to discuss individualized learning but no one ever mentions individualized guidance. Until the correct resources are in place to personally guide students, this nation will remain in crisis mode.

In order to help students relate career interests, develop character, and avoid behavioral problems counselors need an in-depth understanding of what skills are necessary to succeed post high school. This can be accomplished through increased knowledge of pathways in demand, certifications and degrees necessary for a given field, and which colleges or universities offer the training, education, or accreditation for professions with high growth rates.

This is where the government can invest in student capital by ensuring counselors have the training needed for professional development and time available to support students in nurturing talents, learning new skills, identifying abilities and interests, and exploring various passions. Given these are a high school counselors main job functions and they are servicing less students, it is a winning strategy. Personally speaking, if I was given 100-150 students and the role of ensuring success of these students, this is a much more accomplishable goal than the responsibility of 500 students with 50 different duties. Neglecting educational needs leads to an increase in emotional needs and there is nothing a counselor can do about it with so many students to service. It is just a given fact that 80% of the students on a counselor's caseload will get missed. If this issue of student negligence does not get addressed a broken society will become shattered.

Let me offer this scenario. A faucet is leaky, so people offer buckets. The buckets sustain for a little while, but eventually the faucet bursts. So what do people do? Offer more buckets. In comparison, students are not succeeding. Because students are not succeeding mental health issues have escalated. People offer mental health care. This sustains students for a little while, but eventually substance abuse, mental health ailments, and suicide all skyrocket. So what do people do? Build more mental health facilities. This vicious cycle is severely damaging.

Helping students find their niche, knowing there is opportunity and developing a sound plan to achieve goals will not only inspire and motivate students to come to school, but to be an active learner in the process. Helping students see the value in what they are doing should be the main role of a school counselor. The school counseling profession began as a vocational guidance movement and should continue as such.

The Tortuous College Application Process

Students dread the process of applying to college. It appears as though struggling for solutions by creating ineffective strategies has become the norm for the educational industry. By this I mean colleges are continuously scampering to modify websites to obtain more student applicants; on the contrary all the changes have complicated the process hence turning students away. Too much information is exactly that; too much information.

As a result, perspective students are exasperated trying to decipher which information is necessary, what rolling admissions, early admission, direct admissions and regular admissions means, and if they are considered an undergraduate, graduate, future student, or transfer student. The majority of space on a college website is utilized hyper glorifying the college whilst neglecting the basic facts which are essential for students, especially those that have never attended college before. From a personal perspective, I hold a multitude of degrees from varying institutions and also work in the industry and I myself have a difficult time keeping up with these websites because just when I think I understand where to find certain information, it changes.

I get a wrenched feeling in my stomach every time this occurs because now I have to begin the process of learning how to manipulate the website all over again and it becomes exhausting. Eventually, I stop trying because filtering through all the rhetoric has caused me to lose interest. If an educated professional is overwhelmed with all the information and changes, one can only imagine how a perspective student might feel. Arguably, students are tired of wasting time and money applying for colleges they may not even get into.

College applications have become quite costly and many colleges lure students to apply for the mere purpose of boosting data on the number of applicants for that particular school. This process is misleading and unfair to the student. Furthermore, when a student fills out an application for college they believe they need to indicate what program they are pursuing and often students do not know so they become discouraged with the abundance of degree paths offered. Not understanding the process and not knowing one's true desire can cause error on an application.

It has often been said that technology can replace people for more efficiency; all things considered that is not the case with vocational guidance. Students need personal advising to help drive and direct their passions. Even measures that appear simplistic, like locating the application and pressing submit at the end of completing it, can become complicated. Students are unfamiliar with what they have not done and when doing something that involves too much aggravation, they do it with little care and concern or not at all.

Keeping the process simple is one step in keeping kids from shutting down. Helping them to find a career where there is projected job growth is another way to attract college bound students. Getting a degree just to get it no longer serves a purpose when a student graduates can't find a job and has incurred massive student loan debt.

At some colleges certain programs offer direct admittance which means they forgo the 2 year general education requirements and take classes specifically related to a given field. Regrettably, most students are unaware of this option or the process involved. Students need to be better informed on what direct admit means, the competition involved, and what can be done to better prepare for this competition. It seems like a lot of opportunity is missed because information is not being channeled properly.

Students may be interested in a particular program or college and can take classes in high school that better prepare them for what they will need to be successful upon entering college. For example, some students have commented they wish they knew they had to take a specific science or certain level of math because they would have taken it in high school (and actually complete the coursework rather than cheat). By taking it in high school, the student would then have the foundation for that subject matter and could build upon that. In some instances, a student may need certain classes for admission and not realize it until it is too late. This becomes a missed opportunity that could have been avoided if only the student knew.

Another piece turning potential students away from college is the sticker price to attend, which is shocking to say the least. Many advisors assert that is not the bottom dollar, but how are students or parents supposed to know that? It's like going into a store that declares everything is 40% off, why not just mark the items what they should cost instead of trying to trick the consumer into thinking they are getting a bargain. People quickly figure out they are not getting much of a deal and stop shopping at that store, which could be why so many stores are closing.

Students fear student loan debt, so if the cost to attend a certain school is high, students will consider other options before putting forth the energy to bring the cost down of that school. Most students are in search of a decent education, but aren't particularly set on a certain higher education institution, so price can easily deter them. This is especially true for private institutions that cost a lot more.

Dr. Krolczyk

There was one year I had numerous students not apply to a local college because the application process was too complicated. When I tried to explain this to the college, they were offended and didn't want to hear what I had to say. Pride got in the way of assisting perspective students and creating a better process to attract students. As much as I tried to encourage students to apply to this particular university, many were too turned off by the complex process.

Later, when I attended a conference, the president of the college mentioned enrollment was down. Well that sounded about right. Even so, it wasn't worth my time to try and explain why enrollment could be down because my previous efforts were discarded. College officials need to swallow their pride and hear what he public has to say. Part of learning is listening and colleges need to do a better job of that.

I had a student with a 4.0 GPA students contact me and say, "I have started applications for many colleges, but I have a lot of questions about submitting transcripts, choosing what to include in essays, recommendations, and extracurricular." Regardless of how intelligent students are, applying to college is something they have not done before and therefore need a streamlined application process with someone to easily contact for questions. Higher education is a huge investment and availability of professionals to assist with this process is critical in student attainment.

To illustrate this point, think about a first-time home buyer, people don't usually buy homes without looking at them, knowing about the location, market value, and return on investment. More than likely a real estate agent assists with this endeavor and a first-time home buyer may rely on the real estate agent more than someone that has previously gone through the process. The same type of support is needed for students venturing to attend college. Students need help and it is a systematic disservice not to offer it in the capacity in which it is needed.

Most students are completely unaware of what goes into a college application portfolio. There are key sections of information that every college asks for. These include: a high school transcript, ACT/SAT score results, a personal essay (sometimes answering a specific questions on the application), letters of recommendations (usually from teachers and a counselor), and the application itself. As has been noted, when students do not know what is considered for admissions it becomes a guessing game in which case students spread themselves thin. All in all, they may not need to.

For example, a student may not realize having a job can be considered being involved in the community or being good at math is a skill or talent. Through the years, students have been given so much conflicting information they think they do not stand a chance of getting into or succeeding in college. Emphasis should be placed on getting students the correct information so they know where to focus their energy. On the following page is a copy of a personal essay my son wrote and I think it summarizes how a lot of high school seniors feel. I think it is ok not to know what you want to do at seventeen years old. Many adults didn't know at that age how their life was going to be and they turned out just fine.

Student Capital

Brennan Krolczyk

You know that guy who's always there at the right time. They're not incredibly outstanding but they're there when you need them. The guy that stares at a blank computer screen for hours when typing a paper because his mind is in a million different places. The guy who wants to fit in with the crowd but stand out at the same time. That guy is me, Brennan Krolczyk.

I am the oldest of four, I have a dog, and I go to school. I work at Butoku Karate Dojo where I teach kids martial arts. Likewise, I have been training and competing in martial arts for thirteen years. I'm also in the Early College of Macomb program where I take classes at Macomb Community College while still in high school. Impressive, maybe, but these are just the basics. To know me you must know a lot more than a backstory and a couple of personal achievements.

I have been sitting down at my computer for a long time thinking about my goals, dreams and aspirations. In my thinking I have come to the conclusion that I don't know my goals, dreams or aspirations. I don't know who I want to grow up and be, what I want to do, or how I want to do it. The only thing I do know is that I want to be great. No matter what I do in life, I am going to do it to the best of my ability. Now I'm not sure what it is that I'm going to be doing, but whatever it is it's going to be great. Greatness is what moves us all to do better. It's the thing that makes me wake up early and go to school. That strive for greatness is what I am trying to achieve in life. How I will achieve it I don't know yet, but I can tell you the journey is going to be great.

Society needs to stop harassing youths about what they want to be and start helping them discover who they are. They have passions, desires, skills and talents that will be unleashed in time. The more pressure that is placed upon them, the more they turn away. If adults turn their attention the other direction, kids will quietly emerge. They own their passion so it is up to them to find it and dispense it. They are capable, they are willing, yet they just haven't been afforded the opportunity because everyone else is always telling them what they should be doing. Once they figure out who they are, they will then understand which career best suits their personality (Zunker, 2017).

CHAPTER 6
CAREER CONFUSION

"Once a person discovers their passion, they can make a career out of it."

~Dr. Krolczyk

Passion Drives Career Choice

Too often students have a skewed sense of what a particular career actually entails or what is needed to reach a career goal. I had a student I was reviewing career options with and she indicated she wanted to be a nurse. In her mind, she was going to go to college, get in a nursing program, graduate, and get a job. She had a 2.3 GPA and 19 on her ACT. Direct admittance to most nursing programs requires a 3.5 GPA, 24 ACT score, and at least a year of biology and chemistry.

When I asked her which nursing program she was going to get into, she stated "any of them." When I suggested switching a class in her schedule to reflect classes that were more science based, she exclaimed, "I am not really good at science." When I asked her why she wanted to be a nurse, she replied, "I hear there is a need for them and they make good money." Her motive for choosing this particular career did not match her skills and interest. If the student was actually interested in this field, she would have researched it further and if she had, she would have realized nursing is a very competitive program, the application process is quite extensive, and a strong science base is needed to do well in this field. There is a good chance she isn't going to get into a nursing program anywhere.

What is happening is students are so used to getting what they want; the prospect of not getting something they desire doesn't ever cross their mind. That is, until what they want is not within their reach. When this occurs, the conflicting emotions they experience can be overwhelming. That is to say since infancy children have been acclimated to believe all of their desires are within their reach. Kids of this generation have the very best of everything and want for nothing.

The fallacy comes into play when contribution is absent. By not having to work towards things they lack development, growth, and skills which become evident when dealing with disappointment. As a child if dissatisfaction is present, then as an adult frustrations are easier to manage. If the feeling of defeat is being experienced for the first time as an adult, then it is the lack of experience in handling such situations that encompasses the person. This inexperience lends to a lack of confidence.

Self-assurance comes from feeling accomplished; feeling accomplished comes from doing well at something; doing well comes from hard work and dedication, hard work and dedication is applied to things people are interested in. Finding ones interests is instrumental in building confidence. Considering this, students need proper advising, job shadowing, and a back-up plan. The understanding of having to work hard to achieve goals needs to be present.

For example, I have students that want to be engineers, but don't want to take calculus, or students that want to be lawyers, but don't apply themselves in

English. More students are graduating from college without the foundation necessary to perform the basics of anything, let alone a vocation. I am amazed at how many teen drivers do not even know how to pump gas or order food. Why? No one has ever taught them. By someone else always doing these tasks for them they are lacking major life skills. When lacking major life skills, survival away from home at college is a longshot.

It can be very devastating when a student realizes no one is going to just hand them their dream. It is also shocking to find out what the hours and daily functioning of a work schedule are. This is why internships, volunteering, co-ops, and shadowing are critical for students. Not only do these experiences offer realistic expectations, it affords students the opportunity to learn about various career options.

Being exposed to the actual work setting helps students to understand the significance of having a sound knowledge base to perform the functions of the job. It connects what is learned in the classroom to what is needed in the working atmosphere. It adds value to the curriculum. It helps the student to discover that a job entails multiple facets; some pleasant, some not. The image a student has of a career may not resemble the actual duties and function of that career and it is important for students to realize this before investing too much time and money into a career that may not suit their personality.

When students explore careers, they need to take the time to do it thoroughly and not rush. When in a hurry, mistakes are more likely to occur and these mistakes can become quite costly. Understanding fundamentals needed to succeed in a career could alleviate the desire to cheat on academic subjects related to that career. Consequently, many students find themselves taking remedial classes in college because they do not have the prior knowledge needed for a given course.

These remedial classes equate to extra time and money; which can also become added stress. Often, students' claim they may not be interested in a particular class, but what they may not realize is for the career they want to pursue, that particular class may be useful. For example, a student may express interest in pharmacy and not see the relationship between chemistry and medicine. If they did, they would be more likely to invest time and energy into the course work thus preventing them from having to take a remedial course in college.

To put it another way, many classes have relevance for certain fields and students just haven't drawn those connections. That is to say career paths do not inform students enough about which classes are needed for certain professions; students need to learn specific information pertaining to occupations so they can better determine if the track they intend to follow is right for them. However, students are so exhausted from such a strenuous high school curriculum little energy is left for exploration.

Incidentally, many students do not realize applying to an honors college entails a different format and admission criteria. An honors program at the college level does not add things, it replaces. Certain types of students would do well in a program like this while others may not be able to handle it. That being the case, this is where more personalized guidance can prove advantageous.

Wherein lies the issue is the larger the population being serviced is, the longer it takes to service them.

When an attempt is made to offer advice to students in large groups' information becomes muddled. When a lot of information is given at once, little is remembered. Brains are not wired to receive an abundance of material all at the same time. Yet, due to time constraints and budget cuts, more and more schools are resorting to this method of delivery. The educational crisis is partially due to servicing students in mass quantities, which doesn't work and needs to change. As has been mentioned, an incredible amount of undue stress is placed upon today's youth because of poor infrastructure in the schools. It is important to realize that being a teenager in and of itself is a lot pressure whereupon additional tension is not needed.

During the adolescent years, trying to fit in with peers dominates over figuring out what it is they would like to do for the rest of their lives. For this reason, career software programs are not sparking student interests to further research ideas for the future. Considering this, career counselors are needed to help students understand the importance of such career interest software programs and how to utilize results.

Helping students discover who they really are can make a massively daunting task, like career assessment, less nerve-racking. When a task is less intimidating people engage in it more. By engaging more in career inventories, students may stumble upon something that ignites their passion, which will drive them to research programs and scholarships inadvertently working on goals for the future.

Exposing students to careers and pushing careers are completely different objectives. Introducing various professions is ok; telling students at a young age they need to decide what their career goals are is a huge mistake. By the time a student gets to senior year or post high school, they are so besieged with career information they have stopped listening, which is unfortunate because it is during this time they need the information the most. This is what happened to my son with the technology application of checking his grades on his phone. He became so stressed about it, by the time he was in 10th grade, he stopped using the application altogether.

The mistake schools are making is they are not teaching students how to be good students; they are teaching them that college is the only option. This quickly backfires when a student doesn't know how to learn and attends college and fails. Wherefore the student was left to believe this is the only path in life and the perception of life now holds less meaning. Some places of employment will even pay for an employee to obtain an education, but young adults are not aware of this. When they shut down they completely shut down to the point where they cannot even get out of bed.

To start the process on career exploration, discussions about what the student really wants out of life and who they really are needs to be initiated first. A student may have an inclination of what they want to do, but to find out what they are truly passionate about means first-hand experience in the given field. As one student stated, "this internship gave me invaluable experience in conducting academic research, and furthered my love of biology."

People have intrinsic passions that have not yet been unleashed. What this means is there are interests and desires they haven't yet discovered. They haven't revealed a strong feeling for something because they haven't been exposed to it. An intense emotion or enthralling interest could exist and the person just doesn't know it.

Think about food; until a person tries a particular type of food they do not know if they like it or not. As people grow and change, taste buds alter. People can have an underlying interest in something and not even realize it. Trying different things is how they will discover likes and dislikes, fascinations and boredom, talents and shortcomings. Once students figure these things out, they can focus on careers and their future. Contrarily, if they are addicted to electronic mechanisms they will lack the ambition to explore discovery of self.

The Role Career Maturity Plays

A mere fact that is continually being overlooked is that not every student is college bound or ready for college immediately after high school and that's ok. A person can still make a good living without a college education. More conversations need to take place with students on why they want to attend college. Presumably, this will help find the best fit for them post high school. Too many students are going to college, picking a field just to pick one, getting out and not finding a job or not liking that field.

Many students are being redirected to remedial courses because they are not prepared for the rigor of a college curriculum, even if the transcript states differently. Often, students are not mature enough to focus on what they want to do in life. Maturity takes time over a lifespan. Careers unfold through developmental stages coupled with life experiences.

Kids have always been told to get an education or get hands-on training; be that as it may, why can't they get both. Often they need the education to land the job, but the skills needed to perform the duties of the job require hands-on training. The stigma of one or the other needs to stop and an integration of both needs to exist so more people can experience success.

At any rate, everyone is quick to assume kids don't do things because they don't know the *why* and if they did know the *why* they would have a purpose. Even so, knowing *why* they are doing something is not enough; today's youth need to know *how* to do it. Understanding *how* to get from A to B is what will give them meaning in their pursuits.

For instance, an individual may know why they want to go to college, they may even know what career path they want to pursue; but if a person does not know how to apply to college their aspirations will never come to fruition. It is important to realize the significance of what means a person intends on using to fulfill goals. If a person does not know in what manner they intend on doing something guidance may be needed.

Part of the reason there is such disparity between career and education is some students are not developed enough to make these types of decisions. By pressuring them to do so, they just go through the motions without any sense of purpose. Another key point is to let students experience life by paying for things on their own and understanding the basic essentials of survival. They will figure things out if society lets them. By being exposed to hardships, wants, and needs, when the maturity level kicks in, they will have a greater sense of what should be done and how to do it.

Parents contend if they leave kids alone they will do nothing. Ok, so they do nothing. Doing nothing results in getting nothing. Stop paying for your child's car, gas, insurance, spending, sporting events, phone, clothes, Starbucks, X-box live, I-tunes, or Netflix. They will realize real fast that these things cost money and to earn money you need a job. After having multiple jobs they do not like or don't make a lot of money in, they will start career exploring. This time it will be meaningful because they will be doing it by choice.

To enumerate my point, parents of adult kids often say, "I can't wait to get them off my payroll." Consequently, it is the parents that put them on their payroll, so complaining isn't going to change that. Parents want their kids to have a better life than they did which involves being debt free and not having to work hard and struggle. Granted, struggling builds character and debt, if managed properly, builds credit. What is more, parents neglect to understand that even finding a well-paying job after college does not necessarily mean a person will be happy. Happiness is about finding balance, which is why so many parents themselves experience unhappiness.

When someone is always doing for others what they should be doing for themselves, they will never find that balance, which means they will never be truly happy. So while parents think they are helping their child, they really aren't because it involves sacrificing one's own needs. The truth is while parents are busting their tails to pay for the wants their child has, these same children are spending whatever money they do have on frivolous things, which in the long run still leaves them unfulfilled.

Without delay, children should use their money to buy the things they want or have them go without; they will be ok. My two year old thinks I am mean if I don't give him everything he wants. He pouts, cries, and has little fits. Then he gets over it and moves on. Your twenty year old may think you aren't being nice if you don't give them what they ask for, but they too will get over it.

Don't feel bad about it either. Adults need to find

balance in their lives and if that means treating yourself to a pedicure or sporting event and not your teen or adult child, that is alright. You have not done anything wrong and don't let them for a second try to convince you otherwise. Kids question how adults spend their money because adults allow them to. Do not entertain these types of conversations and sooner or later questions of this nature will diminish. Parents need to remember as the adult they are entitled to certain luxuries. I have yet to fathom why some kids have more extravagant items than their parents. The value in that is unclear and on the negative side factors into young adults not wanting to work.

Part of being career mature is exposure to different things so a person can develop emotionally. By participating in various tasks that could lead to perspective careers, a student is more likely to benefit. Listening to speakers, reading what is involved in a job, or watching videos is boring. Kids need to get out into the field or even better, bring it back into the schools. So many beneficial programs for students have been cut.

Have a radio station where kids can practice broadcasting skills, a school newspaper where they can learn more about writing and editing, an auto shop class where they can understand how to take apart an engine and put it back together, construction and woodshop courses where they create things, cooking and sewing classes so they can make things, and business courses so they can comprehend finance. In my 20 plus years of education, I have seen all the courses students love taken away. These include business law, mythology, orchestra, home economics, typing, speech, swim and culinary to name a few. School systems can blame this on funding, but let's be honest, if the funding wasn't there then how have these classes been replaced with AP courses? The truth is it comes down to choice. Extracurricular not only promotes a healthy, stable environment, these courses are truly the heart and soul of a school. For this reason, better course offerings should be top priority.

Many schools have a college representative come to the school to talk about a particular college. Students are then encouraged to visit the college. Along with this, schools should have human resource managers come in and speak to students about a certain industry or place of employment. This would allow students the chance to know exactly what is needed for a particular field.

Schools should also plan/encourage employment visits: go to a courtroom, manufacturer, restaurant, retail, automotive, or hotel. Have students talk with the CEO's and learn firsthand what is involved in running a company, meet the owners, have an understanding of building safety and codes, payroll, and customer service. Additionally, have hiring managers talk to students so they can realize what specific skills are sought after for gainful employment or which colleges they tend to hire from. Allow students the opportunity to ask these professionals questions that could be helpful in their course selections.

Students having a greater understanding of how things works will allow them to make decisions that could ultimately lead to an occupation. However, for schools to do this effectively a person needs to be hired to develop relationships with companies and coordinate the visits, and that should be their only task. As it stands, organizing college visits is not done with grace because it is an additional duty for counselors whom are already overloaded. There is more value in giving people less to do. I think one of the greatest issues with ADHD is people simply have too much to do interfering with their ability to focus. Medication doesn't solve the issue, giving people less to focus on does.

Many students don't realize that there are various skills they may need for a given job. For example, a student may state they want to be a doctor, but not realize they have to specialize in an area, know data and research, computer input, and have an increased understanding of people. Becoming a doctor does not just entail science courses. It is much more involved than that, but many students do not realize this because they are immature.

Some of the most compelling evidence I've garnered regarding students immaturity levels are direct conversations I have had with these young adults. So many of them have told me they want to own a business, yet when I ask them how they are going to fund it, where will it be located, what is the competition, and what will make their business stand out from similar ones, I receive responses along the lines of, "I don't know, I never thought of all that." Being curious about these things sooner, rather than later, will help inspire and motivate dreams.

My daughter has a friend whose mother works at a local dollar store. Her friend's mother knew my daughter was looking for work and attempted to help my daughter get a job there. When I asked my daughter why her friend's mother didn't get her own daughter a job at the dollar store she replied, "Come on mom, seriously, her mom just lets her use her credit card every time she goes out."

The point my daughter was overlooking was rather than the mother working at the dollar store so she can give money to her daughter why not just have the daughter work. This is an extremely valid point because at the same time the mother was working, her daughter was home bored out of her mind constantly texting my daughter to come pick her up so she could hang out. If she was working, she wouldn't be so bored.

One of the reasons keeping busy as a teenager is so important is because the frontal lobe of the brain is not fully developed until the early 20's and development may continue until the age of 25 (Curtis, 2015). In this labile state, growth is evolving and maturity is not complete. During the immature limbic phase, so much in life is to be discovered and learned from the world and about one's self. Without this range, it can be extremely difficult to understand interests. Further, the thought of a rushed decision to decide which career one might want to engage in for the next 20 or 30 years is a frightening thought.

High school graduation can be bittersweet. On the one hand, one is exalted to be free of the conformity of high school and parental authority, joyous of finally being an adult. On the other hand, one quickly realizes adulthood and freedom is not quite as grand as it has been made out to be.

College, career, marriage, home ownership, and a family are all choices that are waiting to be made. These options are not predetermined nor governed by others. Maturity and human growth play a role in this decision-making process, which is why many are unable to comprehend the reality of entering adulthood and linger on codependency.

Encouraging the Skilled Trades

After World War I, the federal government decided to support a career counseling and guidance movement by passing a federal act to assist veterans returning to the workforce. Tests were created to help these veterans find their interests to make choices about educational endeavors and finding ideal jobs. Some of these men returning from war realized pursuit of college was not optimal for them and instead entered the field of skilled trades.

Since they were willing to strive and had the desire to succeed, companies helped mold them. Part of that shaping included having them complete multiple tasks so they had more than one skill set. This type of apprenticeship allowed many to prosper in their field, earning good wages.

An industry that permitted so many families to thrive is now frowned upon by current generations. This turn of events has led to a shortage of talent in the skilled trades. Businesses are constantly ranting, "Can't get anyone to do skill trades and the talent/workforce is drying up. If something isn't done fast we are going to be in a world of hurt." This is due to workers in the manufacturing industry retiring and no one else having the knowledge base to go into these fields. Even though for some students vocation would be their best option, state mandates limit opportunity and availability to explore career technical education classes.

People theorize that no one is going into skilled trades because they don't think they can make a lot of money in these fields. While that concept is interesting in theory, it is not entirely true. The younger generation isn't going into the trades because they don't know enough about this industry. Most of these courses have been cut or minimally offered in the schools. Students are pushed into rigorous classes and little to no room is left in a schedule for anything else.

Student Capital

It infuriates me when I hear comments like, "these young kids are such spoiled little brats they don't want to get their hands dirty." Pardon me, but who allows them the opportunity to get their hands dirty? Most of these kids would love to get their hands dirty, taking things apart and putting them back together, but they are trained to use their minds and not their hands. They aren't allowed to use tools because they are viewed as dangerous. They are constantly told to sanitize and wash their hands. Dirt equals germs and germs are bad. How the hell are they supposed to create if they aren't allowed to explore.

Everyone keeps asking how to get kids more involved in industry. That's easy, expose them to it. Take fieldtrips to manufacturing companies where they can see what these jobs entail. Help them understand that it is not backbreaking, laborious, and boring. It is more of a work-based learning environment where machines do a lot of the creating and people operate the machines. These people are skilled and some even make six figures.

Operating a device, such as a 3-d printer, entails math, computers, design, and engineering. While rethinking education, legislators need to stop forcing kids to take classes that are not for them. Let them find classes that are the right fit so they stay interested in school. Allow a curriculum that taps into their inner passion so they can stay motivated and excel. Help them understand why making a difference in the world matters. Show them how to create a four-year plan that is meaningful. Give students the opportunity to find out what it is they are interested in so they can start doing it. Forcing all students to take college bound classes is screwing our society up.

People go broke trying to look rich because they are unfulfilled in careers and life. The current model in the United States is college first, job after. When people can't find jobs because they don't know what abilities they need to perform these jobs they are all over the place searching for the right fit. What skill is being developed while they learn? Students are so stressed out and bored while learning, they resort to video games and social media for relaxation.

When asked from a human resource director, "what can you do?" many newly graduated students are at a loss for words. This is why apprenticeships are such a critical part of developing career skills. It helps people determine what is needed for a given field, keeps them focused, and offers traits that can significantly contribute to a profession. Furthermore, training helps develop interpersonal and communication skills, which kids of today suck at. Schools need to clearly distinguish between internships and working. Placement in a field of interest is different than working at a fast food restaurant. Yet when kids leave school early to go to work it is called an internship. I notice many Career Technical Education (CTE) courses have capstone in the title. A lot of schools are changing the title of courses to reflect something that the course itself does not entail and this becomes very misleading when creating educational goals.

The belief is that kids need to create educational development plans earlier and younger. This is a difficult task to accomplish because kids don't see the value in it, don't take it serious, and don't understand it. These plans become another item checked off a list that is meaningless to the student. If you think I am wrong, talk to any student that has been forced to take an interest inventory as part of their educational development plan. The key word is forced.

Most kids don't want to think about their future when they are still going through puberty and trying to understand hormonal changes in their body. This is also a critical time for adolescents to figure out how to balance school work, social lives, and extracurricular activities. They seek clarity in the meaning of life, their heritage, faith, and wonders of the world. They have yet to master the art of speaking to one another. They are unsure how to articulate thoughts, express feelings, or take measures that constitute good manners. They are curious about natural disasters, terrorism, and poverty. There are so many uncertainties in the world around them and yet they are pressured to determine what they want to do for the rest of their life.

Educators have long noted that social impact on people's lives does influence productivity. What do teenagers really know about socialism and family structure? Numerous people have overcome barriers and succeeded. Ultimately, prospering comes down to desire.

Those that want to accomplish something bad enough will find a way. Others will use every obstruction possible as a crutch as to why they couldn't reach their goal.

Human behavior can be fascinating and enabling all at the same time. What people fail to realize is that everyone has baggage; some just carry it better than others. Everyone has fears and anxiety; some just face these emotions while others avoid them. All people have passions; some have discovered these feelings while others are still searching what it is they are enthusiastic about.

In my graduate level course on career counseling, students reflected on their own journey and here's what some of them had to say:

"I went into things I presumed society wanted me to go into, like jobs that made financial sense. I put who I really was on the back burner. A mistake I will never make again. I feel when people follow their passions, certain energy is created inside them, and things will work out because they are working with who they are. To do this though, takes courage and fortitude."

"It is a fact though that 85 percent of the American public hate their jobs. I feel many of them have their job by default, in other words, they are working it because they feel like they have to."

"I was going to become a CPA because I have always been good with numbers but I decided that I no longer wanted to work at a job that I can do, I wanted to be fulfilled."

"I would wake up, dreading having to go to work in the morning. I did not want to feel the pressure of the job. My body physically hurt from the stress. I had to stop the job because my coping mechanisms were not working well anymore, and the stress was beginning to eat me alive. I could actually feel the pressure eating away at my body, like a slow burning acid."

"Often times, I felt like I wanted to quit and find alternative employment where I felt validated. It was as if more and more requirements were placed on my plate, with impossible timelines to complete the tasks. It was overwhelming and perpetuated the depression. I already felt overwhelmed and feeling inadequate that I could not complete all the tasks on-time made me questions my abilities."

Student Capital

When I read these testimonies of how people felt regarding their careers it instantly reminded me of how students feel that hate school; trapped, stressed, overwhelmed, impossible to keep up, depressed, and questioning their abilities. All I could think of is how we get people in a better place so they do not feel so hopeless; and the answer is student capital.

Vocational and job-ready skills used to be taught with reading, writing, and arithmetic. This included wood working, metal shop, welding, cooking, and other common sense everyday living abilities. Kids were happy, enjoyed school, and were well prepared for life. Then theory changed and the curriculum became focused on preparing every student for a college track. This included taking more academic related classes and less occupational training.

As a result of this pendulum swing, kids have become anxious, hate school, and are totally unprepared for life. Instead of resorting to traditional methods where kids enjoyed education, schools have taken a more aggressive approach pressuring teachers to engage in more rigorous instruction. This approach is counterintuitive, harmful, and dividing. Kids are depressed, parents are overburdened, and kids are in constant competition. The culture of schools, as early as elementary, has become toxic.

Some of the backlash society is seeing stemmed from concerns of higher socio-economic status or certain ethnicities having an advantage point in learning. So, to be fair and consistent, all students started being groomed for a college career path. This concept became known as "no child left behind" and "closing the educational gap." Not everyone, however, is suited for this type of rigorous track because a huge factor overlooked was maturity.

Many students do not excel in traditional subjects and have no desire to expand academic horizons during their high school years. That's not to say they never will, they just are not ready at that time. Certain students may be much more comfortable in a mechanical or artistic setting instead of enamored with college level prep work. Some students thrive in a studio or workshop as opposed to a lecture hall or traditional classroom. Not everyone attends college or even cares about college.

The extreme force and pressure of higher level

courses has deterred kids emotionally, intellectually, and physically; indeed leaving several students behind. Now kids are graduating high school neither prepared for a vocational or academic setting and yet legislation refuses to heed this warning. Fewer students are benefiting from a college degree, but since industrial classes continue to be cut and college preparatory classes continue to rise; the only path students are led to follow is going to college.

This infrastructure has caused a high failure rate, underemployment, increased depression, and uncertainty about the economic future. While the manufacturing sector is growing, finding qualified individuals is shrinking. Student debt is at an all-time high, job growth for college educated individuals is diminishing and what is left is a country in chaos; lying, stealing, and killing one another.

If students were allowed to choose pathways that led to stimulating and productive careers, they could prosper as adults. A person with a lucrative profession is less likely to engage in immoral behavior. Having solid, transferable skills keeps people grounded. What a greater place it would be for all of us if the modern educational system and workplace can join forces to provide this type of stability for our children. The college for everyone mentality needs to dissipate and individualized post high goals needs to exist instead.

The staple of high school learning is exploring what you are good at coupled with what you enjoy and making a living doing it. Guiding students in turning passion and skills into employment is where schools should be focused. Whether it entails a 4 year college, 2 year college, certification, or trade, students need assistance in how to pursue their objective so their imagination, inventiveness, and originality can soar.

I recently read an article in Forbes magazine where it mentioned the economy's problem with skilled trade is a mismatch; people do not think a career of this nature can be well-paid and if they knew how much they could make, they would go into fields such as welding, carpentry, electrical, plumping, etc. This came from CEO's and CFO's. How many high school students were surveyed? If I had to guess, I would say none.

Not thinking they can earn a decent living is only a small part of the problem; the bigger issue is they don't know anything about these fields and don't feel confident they can learn what is needed to perform these types of jobs. Ever since skilled trades have been reduced in the schools, students know little to nothing about this type of industry. Even the technology needed to strive for excellence in manufacturing, is not the same type of technology offered in the schools. If allocation of school funding is going to be spent for technology shouldn't it be spent on technology that is most useful to the student? Accessibility of these classes in the school system is the bigger issue.

An aspect that is constantly overlooked is the skilled trades courses that schools still do have available can have limited space, so the course fills up quickly. Or students can't fit these electives in their schedule because those slots are used to retake failed required classes. For example, if a student fails a foreign language and this subject is required for graduation, they may have to place it back in their schedule multiple times until they pass it, thus inhibiting the prospect of taking other courses. Having to repeat courses can cause major strain on a student. This additional tension is one factor why kids cheat.

I had one student that was a senior in high school and failing English. His entire schedule consisted of all academic classes due to previously failing some required classes. He wanted to take design and engineering, but couldn't fit it in his schedule. As if that wasn't stressful enough, he now had the looming threat of possibly not graduating if he didn't pass all his classes.

So, before the end of a card marking, he went to the teacher and asked for handouts of missing work. Since it is now a reflection of the teacher if a student does not do well, the teacher gave him all his work. The student then text messaged some friends to "send him the answers" and in one day completed his missing assignments to bring his grade up to a passing mark.

He manipulated the system and was alright with this because, as he explained, "I had no choice. I have to pass or I won't graduate and my homework load in all my classes is too much it is impossible to keep up, I go to work every day after school." He made a moral decision based on what he felt needed to be done so he could succeed; he equated success to getting his diploma. This student is not unique in his thinking; cheating has become the norm among the student population.

So now the unanswered question becomes what is society going to do since the talent work force is drying up? Parents don't always want kids to go into manufacturing because they fear a dim future, yet these trade skills are in high demand. Parents misconceive how much job security exists in a field such as electrician, welder, or plumber where they can name their price, make top dollar, and enjoy what they do. However, there are times when parents do want kids in these types of courses, but offerings are limited.

Once again, not everyone is college bound and that is alright. What is important is that a person finds the "right fit." The best way to do this is to try different things to see what a student might like so they can determine if they are good at some of these tasks. If a person isn't interested in the trade, they will never develop their skills. However, if it is something that makes them happy, they will continually strive to improve. The better they become at it, the more opportunities they will have, the more opportunities they have, the more money they can make.

What is needed is for students to learn about the manufacturing industry so they can assess if they are interested in these fields. This may be a difficult feat because these types of programs have been reduced in most schools. Clearly these classes need to be brought back because elimination of these programs has impacted our society beyond belief.

Look at a class like auto shop; not every kid might become a mechanic, but I can assure you every kid will eventually have a car. Shouldn't they know the basic functions of that car? Also, it is much more difficult to cheat in a class where you are graded on what you do rather than what you know. Demonstrating how to change the oil is different than answering multiple choice questions on it.

The best way to enhance enrollment in courses pertaining to skilled trades is to reconstruct state graduation requirements. It is taking a toll on pupils and some of these requirements are not relevant to every student. It is difficult for a student to reach a level of balance and momentum when mandates are one-sided. More diversity needs to exist among course options so students will be less stressed and have more of a desire to come to school.

Since there is such a huge demand for skilled trades in the workforce, students should not be pushed into advanced placement or early college which can cause an undue amount of stress and anxiety. Pushed, bullied, coerced whatever you want to call this type of behavior it is disingenuous and needs to change. Listen, I am not saying no student should ever take an advanced or accelerated class; there are some students that need the challenge and do extremely well in classes of this structure. I am saying students should not be led to believe that if they don't engage in such rigor they will never accomplish anything in life because that simply is not true.

Educational institutions need to seriously reconsider the infrastructure of facilities to be more conducive for programs like auto, welding, woodshop, and culinary. A student can learn critical life skills from these courses while exploring the potential for a career. Federal and state funding needs to be doled out to schools so this can happen. More money is being spent being reactive to crisis situations than being proactive helping individuals find a sense of accomplishment so they don't lose their mind and resort to drastic measures. Look at how many students are being medicated for disorders. I would feel confident in saying our nation has reached an all-time high of stressed out anxious unhappy teens.

If a restructuring of the curriculum is not put into place; American students are going to experience a huge fallback. Look at the disconnect they have in speaking skills. There exists a generation of socially awkward teens, yet a communications course is not required for graduation. Kids don't learn as well from webinars or online tools and don't know how to ask for help.

These kids become adults who still don't ask questions. Instead, they post on social media how fabulous their life is, which is the furthest from the truth. To be successful, students need to be able to balance the viral world with the real world. Complicated systems don't work in the real world so things need to be kept simple so skills can be acquired. When an economy is more skilled, it produces higher results for everyone.

Today's generation of kids are so consumed with academics that little to no time is left for basics; like knowing how to rake leaves, shovel snow, mow the lawn, or change a light bulb. When asked to write a personal essay for college on challenges they have encountered, they are bewildered on what to write because they have had little to no hardships.

College representatives and employers want to know that if they hire or admit someone, that person can persevere through struggles. Furthermore, many human resource departments have stated seeking prospective employees that can balance practical knowledge and formal knowledge; street smarts and intelligence.

Some of the top traits employers look for:

1. Intelligence and endurance.
2. Person that is not easily intimated.
3. The courage to take on new projects.
4. Ambition to grow in careers.

A person, whom has not experienced real learning and tends to stress easily, usually lacks confidence and is viewed as lazy. This type of person will have a difficult time finding and keeping employment. There is a desperate need to go back to the drawing board when employable skills were taught in schools. I can remember taking sewing, typing, shorthand, home economics, wood-shop, and auto shop in middle school and high school.

My school also had a radio station that I loved being part of. There also existed opportunities to attend a vocational school. This is a quickly growing technologically driven society, where everything is wanted instantaneously without putting forth any effort. Rather than have people conform to society, civilization has given in to the demands of people, and it has wreaked havoc on the country.

How state legislators have not been able to draw the connection between the increase in mental instability, decrease in elective offerings, and decrease in manufacturing awareness is beyond me; but a common theme you will note throughout this book is they need to address these issues and fast. I also question how leaders in our nation have not discovered the widespread cheating occurring in schools. Students think this is ok because a system has been set-up that is impossible to master; so a perception that it is being mastered is offered instead.

So much pressure is placed upon so many people; no one is willing to say anything. Well, now I am speaking out because the United States of America's educational system cannot continue this fallacy; it is destroying youths. The possibility of being a country where opportunities exist, based on accomplishments regardless of one's prominence, is being abolished. This concept was once known as *The American Dream*!

CHAPTER 7

SCARE OF COLLEGE DEBT

"You must gain control over your money, the lack of it will forever control you."

~Dave Ramsey

Financial Aid is not Entirely Free

One of the nation's biggest concerns is the rise in tuition and college debt. Since allocations to higher education have been cut, many universities resorted to increasing tuition rates as a means of supplementing the income lost. This has left students with enormous amounts of debt that are difficult to pay back. College graduates fear that companies may not want to hire them due to significant loan debt.

Making college a less affordable option only deters people from investing in their future. When people realize something is so far out of reach because of how much it costs, they become despondent. Goals and ambitions are quickly crushed. Public policy and attitude need to change if kids of today are going to even stand a chance for a better tomorrow.

Students are naïve and vulnerable and often taken advantage of. For example, students need to be cautious of the aggressive marketing approach colleges are taking to boost rankings. This includes recruiting with the intent of denying. It makes the college appear more selective, but costs the student money because they have to pay to apply. If a student has a limited amount of money for college applications and is wasting it on colleges they don't stand a chance of getting into, this presents a problem; emotionally and financially.

Parents and students alike tend to misunderstand the purpose and process of applying for financial aid. Having students better educated on how this resource can assist in paying for college is an effective strategy in empowering families. Free Application for Federal Student Aid (FAFSA) is an online form that needs to be completed and submitted (the link is listed in Appendix A).

Many institutions prefer a student to apply for FAFSA before doling out scholarship money. The reason for this is because a college or university would like to know if the student is eligible for any federal student aid. Scholarship award can then be based on what a student might still need to cover tuition. The federal aid and scholarship amount may not cover costs in its entirety, but certainly can help. Many colleges have a scholarship fund from which they are able to pull additional monies if necessary to assist a deserving student.

If a student were to take a loan out, repayment options can be extremely confusing. Borrowing money isn't necessarily a bad thing because it is considered investing in one's future. However, a student still needs to be cautious of how much is being borrowed and the ability to pay it back. Students should only borrow what they need and a financial aid expert at the college can explain how to do that.

A student needs to take the time to sit down with a financial aid adviser and discuss his/her particular situation and formulate a plan sooner rather than later on how to cover the astronomical cost of a college education. Emails and phone calls are not as concise as a face-to-face conversation. Seek out the financial aid office at a perspective college and ask for an in-depth explanation of your reward letter. A reward letter is what is sent by the financial aid office of a college or university and it explains how much is given as a grant and how much is available to a student as a loan. There is no shame in not knowing, the only disgrace is pretending to know something when you don't.

One of the greatest complaints of this generation is students have no comprehension of finances, yet the expectation is to take out large sums of money and repay it. How is a student supposed to do that when they lack basic concepts of money? Do government agencies really wonder why the student loan debt is so massive? Not only should finance be a required course in high school, colleges too should require a course in cost, expenses, budget and savings. If an organization affirms they are invested in students, then they need to start showing it. Students will be more trusting when genuine behavior is modeled.

Educating every student on money matters is the best way to demonstrate a moral commitment to student outcome. Student capital needs to begin somewhere, so if an organization is not going to invest in students, then the student needs to invest in himself. One way a student can do this is to become familiar with definitions pertaining to the FAFSA. Below are some basic financial aid terms:

EFC expected family contribution
SAR student aid report send via email (read over and correct)
COA cost of attendance (estimated) colleges are calculating this
Direct Expense – must pay i.e.: tuition
Indirect Expense- still need i.e.: books

So, how is the financial aid amount determined? The estimated direct expenses + estimated indirect expenses = cost of attendance. The expected family contribution (EFC) is subtracted from the cost of attendance (COA) to estimate an award amount and an award notification letter is sent to the student. This should be read over carefully before signing and returning. Students should also take into consideration the following:

*Available aid is unique to each college based on COA.

*Transfer students do not get same amount of money as incoming freshman.

*FAFSA uses the custodial parent's income.

*Scholarships are separate from FAFSA.

*Local scholarships = smaller pool of applicants.

*Attending a financial aid information session.

*Attending a FAFSA Workshop (to help fill out the application).

*Attending an award letter workshop.

*Work <u>with</u> your student- not <u>for</u> your student

If a family has more than one child in college, the parent only needs one FAFSA ID, but each child needs their own. If you don't need a loan- don't take one out. When students complete college they want to do exciting things because they are tired of living the daily ins and outs of being a college student; this is difficult to do when paying back loans. It would behoove a high school to have someone available for the sole purpose of assisting with these forms and the process. Parents and students have a lot of questions and based on how they reply to some of the questions on the application, monies awarded can be impacted.

What exactly is a financial aid packet? Financial aid is doled out from the higher education institution. Once a FAFSA application is complete, each school listed will send an award letter with a financial aid packet. This packet includes possible money from federal, state, and institutional sources. It is based on the cost of attending the school and individual needs. Therefore, different schools will have varying offers.

A student can compare the aid packages to determine which school is the most affordable. For example, one college may offer more money than another, but what that student may not realize is the college that offered more money costs more to attend. Therefore, a student should look at the money he/she would have to pay out to determine which deal is the best option.

It is also important when listing colleges on your financial aid form to list in order of preference. Colleges use this preference list to determine the seriousness of student interest. A student is likely to get the most aid amount from the first and second choices listed on a FAFSA form.

When a student receives an award letter, they should make an appointment with the college's financial aid office to review the terms and conditions. Every higher education institution has an office specifically dedicated to the financial aid process. These people are experts in assisting student with this procedure. Since policies continue to change, this department would have the most current information. For example, students can now apply for FAFSA in October of senior year and utilize tax returns from 2 years ago.

Before this change, students and parents would estimate what the tax return would be, then go back and adjust it once taxes were actually filed. This alleviates the back and forth. Merit based cannot be adjusted because it reflects a student's academic standing, but need based refers to financial circumstances and can be adjusted. Students can discuss individual conditions with a financial aid officer at the college. This is a free service and not utilized as much as it should be.

Dr. Krolczyk

Deadlines for FAFSA and scholarships are set so colleges can determine the amount of students applying and how much to award. Keep in mind, a student may apply past a given school deadline, but may not be considered for the maximum amount. To be given the most consideration, students should apply as soon as possible. To find out a schools deadline, please visit that schools website or the FAFSA site. If there are special considerations, like a parent's death, or a student supporting him/her self, the financial aid office can assist with the best way to report this on the form.

Many high schools offer financial aid nights, which is a great opportunity to receive information about the process. A lot of community colleges offer assistance with filling out the form. Some high schools or colleges offer informational sessions on how to interpret the award letter. All of these are great opportunities with becoming more familiar with financial planning for college. When in doubt, ask, and continue to ask until you get a greater understanding of priority consideration and what your child may be eligible for. The knowledge you gain can prove to be invaluable.

Student Capital

Since high schools do not have a financial aid adviser at their schools, it is highly encouraged that students find out as much as possible about this endeavor. Quite honestly, that could be one of the best investments a school system can make. Investing in students doesn't mean having the latest and greatest technology available, rather using the appropriate platform to service their needs. Having an expert on site that can answer questions, meet with families, and explain or review the process would motivate so many students to apply for college.

So, until school systems realize the value in employing such an agent, families are left to their own devices. Thankfully, the FAFSA website is very user friendly and easy to manipulate. Just beware of potential scams. Financial aid is a free process and no one should ever have to pay for this service. Sometimes families are in such a rush to check this off the list they get taken advantage of. Slow down and go through the process correctly.

Dr. Krolczyk

Scholarship Chaos

Applying for scholarships can be a fulltime job which requires research, time, and perseverance. Like anything worthwhile, work needs to be applied to reap the benefits. Thousands of dollars each year go unused because students are not aware of what types of scholarships exists or are too lackadaisical to fill out the applications.

On the positive side, students that do apply have an advantage because less competition exists. Students tend to think applying for scholarships is a lot of work, but that is not necessarily true. Most applications ask simple questions like extracurricular activities, work experiences, special awards, and/or career goals. An essay on a specific topic or personal essay may also be required.

Most students already have a personal essay from college applications. What is important to remember is the essay is an opportunity for college representatives to get to know more about them; everyone has accolades but personal experiences vary and that is what a personal essay should reflect; an attribute of the person's life. This is a student's opportunity to share their story, likes and dislikes and challenges, strengths, weaknesses, and thoughts and feelings on life. It should be sincere and meaningful.

There are different venues for scholarships and some of these include university related, local, and national. The university funding is mostly merit-based, but not always. There are other scholarships available such as hardship, family alumni, leadership, multicultural and program based scholarships. Financial assistance sometimes is available for students in unique situations that perhaps don't qualify for federal support. Such exceptions and dollar amounts are different for each college, so students need to explore options, procedures, and deadlines for applying.

The deadlines have become somewhat conniving as some institutions have the cutoff date, for some of the best scholarships, listed as early fall of senor year. This is an injustice to students as many of them have not determined a specific college yet or are not aware of such stringent time limits. This leads one to believe the college is not sincere in offering money for a student to help fund their educational endeavors. Regardless, students need to take the time to peruse these deadlines.

Many higher education institutions do have money on reserve and can allocate more to a given student if needed, but often is not aware of a student's financial circumstances. This is another reason why students need to have better communication skills; so they can properly advocate for themselves and inquire about additional funding. Students should bargain with financial aid representatives at a given college.

For example, if a student is offered more money at one college, but really wants to attend a different one, they should ask for the same award package. If a representative senses this is the determining factor in that student attending that college, they may match or exceed the award package offered at a competitive college. It never hurts to ask.

Local scholarships are usually found through the schools and include local businesses, charitable organizations, or private donors. However, school personnel get busy and do not always list them all. Attempting to better utilize technology, many schools have resorted to links or websites, which muddle information causing students less accessibility. It is always baffling why a process as important as scholarships is not given more attention. Clearly, students need more face-to-face guidance on scholarship procedures. This is why scholarship advocacy should become school policy and an inherent part of school aid funding.

Due to such high caseloads, school counselors are not able to foster relationships with all students whereas scholarship direction can be offered. Therefore students need to seek prospects on their own. Numerous local entities are stumped as to why more students do not apply for monies being given for college sponsorship. There have been times the schools have been contacted by the endower to seek a prospective recipient.

Undoubtedly this is indicative of poor representation from the school. I recall once asking for access to list local scholarships on a district site and I was denied this capability. One person for the entire district is the only one that had access and since scholarships were not their only duty, several scholarships probably never got added or updated. A distributed leadership style needed to exist so information was properly channeled and dispersed. Students may not even realize that they can, and should, apply for more than one local scholarship.

Another venue students can use to seek scholarships is national scholarships. Nationwide scholarships are usually listed with high schools, but students can also pursue these on their own though online resources. Students just need to be careful with personal information given out, advertisements or newsletters inadvertently signed up for, and scams. One student mentioned an abundance of emails being sent to her by a database used to seek potential national scholarships. Not all scholarships were applicable to her and it simply took too much time to decipher which ones were and which ones were not. So she had to delete that email account.

Nationwide scholarships are usually filtered, so a student should carefully read terms and conditions before applying. This can become time consuming, but can also save a student a lot of money. Students waste a lot of time on social media sites, so investing in their future is a better utilization of their energy.

Students tend to deter from private colleges because of the high cost. Almost every representative I have spoken to from a private college suggests a lot of opportunities for scholarships to bring down expenses; however, most students do not know this. The "sticker price" is beyond their affordability, so they do not consider that college an option.

Some private colleges have brought the cost down so much it could potentially end up more affordable than a public school. I have seen expenditures brought down by almost half of the listed price to attend. If a student is interested in attending a private college, they should probe more about financial opportunities.

Where the disconnect exists is sometimes a student is not that passionate about that particular school, so to exhaust themselves seeking additional money can be befuddling which discourages students from trying. I know colleges uphold that if the student isn't fervent about attending then that is not the type of student they want to enlist. In all reality, students are not enthusiastic about many things today and it is a huge mistake for the college to have that kind of mindset. The cost of college is so excessive students have grave concerns about attending any university. They continually wonder if they will receive a return on their investment.

Colleges have mechanisms to assist students in determining affordability. In fact, being part of a school organization like Health Occupations Students of America (HOSA) or Distributive Education Clubs of America (DECA) can earn students additional money. Some universities recognize a student's affiliation with these clubs as evidence of dedication and achievement and may offer an increase in merit-based award money. Students should inquire from admission representatives what other options or grants may be available.

Students also need to be cognizant of scholarships that are renewable, automatic, or one -time. A school might indicate a student will receive x amount of dollars every year for 4 years, but the student may have to reapply every year to get that money, or apply to the college by a certain date (usually fall of senior year). If it is an automatic scholarship, then there is nothing the student needs to do. A one-time scholarship refers to the money being given once and that is it. Stipulations and guidelines vary from college-to-college and scholarship-to-scholarship; which is why reading the information in great detail and asking questions is important. This information is not always as clear as it should be.

Many colleges also have what is known as a cost calculator where a student can determine what the cost of their college education will be. The problem is no one tells students this or shows them how to utilize this tool. High school and college officials need to keep in mind students have never gone through this process before so it is all new to them. Often, they do not know what to ask. Since most scholarship applications have deadlines, students can inadvertently miss these deadlines which can significantly impact possible grants.

Good politics can equal bad policy. More pressure on students to find monies to fund their education leads to heightened stress and anxiety. Although people do underestimate scholarship opportunities, there is little guidance in seeking these prospects. This needs to change if the United States does not want to remain a nation with massive student loan debt. Students are sometimes oblivious because connections with school staff are limited, if existent at all.

Students also need to be aware of scams. Scholarships give money, so a student shouldn't have to sign up for something, attend a seminar, or pay anything to be considered for the endowment. Never at any time should a credit card or bank information be given. Lots of misleading scholarships are listed as a method to collect information on students so services can be solicited or identities stolen.

Schools do not always filter through these when they list scholarship opportunities either, so parents and students need to read information carefully. When caseloads were smaller and tasks were fewer, counselors invested a lot of time into looking at links and websites of scholarships prior to listing them. However, that is no longer possible so whatever is sent to a school is listed without any reviewing. Because it is listed, parents and students think it is legitimate. The sad reality everyone is so busy no one has time to do things properly.

The 3 basic types of awards most commonly offered are:

Merit Based

Award money given for academic accomplishments.

Need Based

Award money based on financial need.

Non Need Based

Award money without regard for merit or financial need.

Anything else a person should be leery of. Stay away from scholarships that encourage becoming a member to qualify for the award. This is often a strategy used to build affiliations with the company under the guise of scholarship offerings. The bottom line is a student can use multiple resources to aid in paying for college, but needs to be diligent in seeking these opportunities. A student that waits to seek opportunities can miss out on a lot of money.

Job Outlook

Every time I hear of a student graduating college but not getting a job I ask what the job outlook was for that career path and I almost always get a bewildered look. A job outlook is projected growth in a given job field. Students are naïve enough to think that just because a college offers a degree in a field there are also jobs in that same field. Of course, this is not the case hence the massive student loan debt the nation faces.

A former student of mine graduated with a degree in x-ray technician, has yet to find a job utilizing this degree, and is currently working 4 different part time jobs just to make ends meet. He concluded there are too many people in this field and not enough jobs. I had another student that graduated with a law degree, passed the bar exam, but is working at a dealership. There are so many variables when prospecting a career and students need to be aware of what these variables are prior to embarking on a career path. When students hear of former students not finding employment, they become discouraged and start to lose faith in the scholastic system.

Student Capital

As can be seen better career guidance is needed in higher education. Projection of future job growth should guide degree paths and students should be given assistance in determining which paths those are. This detrimental step is missing and by being obsolete students are undergoing unnecessary agony.

Many people are not aware that during the mass higher education era, the baby boomers started their university education and once they were done, they started taking jobs in the fields that they have studied. Currently, the standard of living is so expensive many seniors cannot afford to retire, so they hang on to their jobs for as long as they possibly can. This means that students graduating from college may not have an open spot available in their field of study.

Unfortunately, one of the reasons elders cannot afford to retire is because of the desire to overcompensate for their children thus creating more financial stress upon themselves. Another reason is the high cost of medical maintenance. Many seniors spend their entire savings on healthcare; which is not how life is supposed to be. Like college, medical upkeep has become astronomical and impossible to fund.

Aside from people holding on to their jobs longer, programs are not specific. Again, going back to earlier times, a person studied an area and became an expert in it. The knowledge gained was specific, focused, and intentionally related to what a student would be doing in the field. Currently, too many generic degree programs exist and industry is finding student graduates that are not specialized or even capable because not enough direct knowledge was obtained. Such broad degrees are almost meaningless.

CHAPTER 8
HIGHER EDUCATION DEBACLE

"Everything should be made as simple as possible, but not simpler"

~Albert Einstein

College Readiness

During earlier times, it was believed young people should obtain a liberal education before attending college because "that education should cultivate the intellectual virtues useful for any of life's endeavors," (Kisker, 2010, p.183). The belief was that students were not yet qualified for university education and needed more guidance for higher learning and higher level thinking.

Currently, many students enter a higher learning institution directly from high school. Some succeed, others drop out. When speaking with a former student that dropped out of college, he indicated that he slept through most of his classes in high school, even the AP classes, and still graduated with above a 4.0 GPA. Going on to college, he then proceeded to fail most of his college courses his freshman year. He blames the school system suggesting, "high schools do virtually nothing to prepare students for the future," then added, "My brother was also a substitute teacher and was nothing more than a glorified babysitter and when he actually did try to instill some hard truths and life lessons into his students, he was fired for it."

This same student took some time off, worked some odd jobs, and tried to figure out what it was he wanted in life. Once he realized how he wanted his future to unfold, a desire was created within him to take action to get what he wanted through hard work and creative invention. He reapplied to college and is currently excelling in all his classes. This is because sometimes what people believe translates to how they feel, and how they feel drives behavior. When behavior is driven in certain directions, it can yield amazing results.

On the flip side of the proverbial coin, pressure from administrators and politicians to raise high school graduation rates give students a misconceived notion about academic progress. Since educational leaders are continuously being told to raise graduation rates and reduce failure rates the message becomes obvious; legislators want students passing and getting good grades. This has been interpreted to mean if they miss a deadline, extend the deadline. If work is tuned in late, give them full credit. If a test yields a low score, let them retake it without penalty. The bottom line is to offer multiple chances to pass and raise their grade; which is not realistic in nature.

Today's generations of students are much different than previous generations. This generation appears to be further behind when it comes to accountability and maturity. By this I mean if a student fails, they blame the teacher, if they pass they assert the success was all on their own. They have difficulty accepting constructive criticism and correcting their work, which is why they have difficulty entering the workforce.

This generation is unwilling to spend countless hours doing work, if they fail they give up rather than sacrificing, failing, and trying harder. When a program becomes too complex, students tune out rather than try to figure it out. By tuning out, they are left frustrated. Because they are frustrated they feel inferior. To compensate for feelings of inferiority, they knock others down. This manipulative behavior of knocking others down is so they can feel superior. This vicious cycle starts by achievement being devalued. Students feel lost and when they feel lost they feel like they have no control. When there is no control, there is less performance.

One way to help this lost generation learn is to show examples of things. If a concept is presented in a concrete way, it becomes more memorable. Another effective method is engagement. Doing something contributes to muscle memory. Finally, when learning is enjoyable, a person is more apt to pay attention.

The diagram below illustrates a three-fold process of learning. Tender learning is during the earlier years, power struggle is mid-year, and mature learning is in later years. A person must first come to appreciate learning, will encounter undesirable experiences with it, but as they grow and develop will heal those wounds to once again be able enjoy learning.

Dr. Krolczyk's Process of Learning

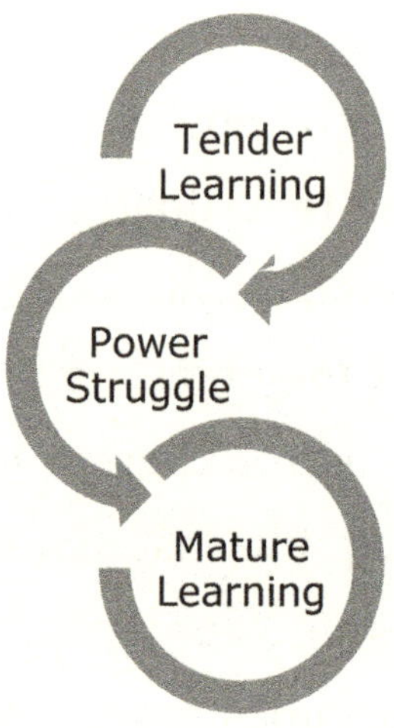

When you consider tender learning think about the elementary years. During this time, learning is unconscious. The goal is to attract students to learning. Everything is presented in a positive, encouraging, playful way. Sort of like romantic love when people first meet and fall in love. Then there is the power struggle. This is an unconscious reaction to negative learning experiences. This can be viewed as similar to negative experiences in a relationship. A person may be wounded during this phase, but through hard work and dedication, growth and healing can take place. Healing entails awareness. Mature learning is the conscious experience of profound knowledge. Once a person has a taste of how satisfying this can be, they want more of it. Similar to when a marriage is flourishing.

Tender Learning-unconscious-positive
Power Struggle-Unconscious-negative
Mature Learning-conscious-satisfying

Admission Barriers

First and foremost when deciding to attend college, students need to acquaint themselves with admission criteria so they are not misled. Just because a college sends a student personalized literature doesn't mean the student has a chance of getting accepted. Anxiety is heightened as students anticipate hearing from a college that made them feel wanted, yet never had any intent of admittance. Arguably, the student gets their hopes up only to be let down and rejected.

Student Capital

A prospective college student may believe the college is truly looking at them as a good fit because the institution sends personalized information. What the student doesn't realize is information was obtained from tests taken and is more generic than specific. Just as disheartening is when colleges indicate having specific criterion, but accept any and all students that apply. When a student no longer feels chosen or has a looming sense of deception, they lose interest in attending that college.

It is helpful to have students talk to other students already attending a particular college because they have lots of insight to offer. Think of how when a person is in the market to buy a new home, they may talk to a possible neighbor already living where they want to move to find out what the area is like. Sometimes a family might visit the community to see what it is like. Incoming students need to do the same for college campuses. They should take the time for a guided tour and even walk around on their own.

When doing so, they should try to picture themselves as a student there. It's ok to be undecided as many colleges offer numerous programs. Finding the right atmosphere is what will be critical to their success. This might help in retaining students as well. I know 2 students this year that plan on transferring back home because the college campus was not what they thought. Neither of the students visited the campus prior to attending.

Kids have resources, but need the relationships with people to show them how to use these resources. This component is significantly lacking in high schools. To state the obvious, every staff member is so overloaded and burnt out, they are inaccessible to students. This is a huge mistake because then kids resort to the internet and have a tendency to believe everything they come across is true.

Ideally, there should be a mandatory course in high school which incorporates learning about degree paths in higher education, skilled trades, certifications, and job outlook. Doing things that matter with kids is significant in overcoming existing barriers. Having class assignments that incorporate applying to these programs would be most beneficial to kids as there exists a lot of confusion.

Schools systems promise to offer all sorts of advising, but the system is not set up to permit this. Essentially, they are promising to do things they are not equipped to accomplish.

Counselors and teachers are inundated with paperwork for reporting purposes; they are not able to focus on the individual student or students as a whole. Basic needs, like how to apply for scholarships, are not being met and this is a huge disadvantage to students. The additional burdens placed upon school personnel, and lingering stress, is transparent to the student body resulting in germane questions being suppressed.

An additional burden teachers currently face is teaching up to the bell. This is horrible pressure because the end of the hour is when most teachers have an opportunity to talk or connect with kids. Time left at the end of class can also be spent with students socializing with one another or even getting a head start on homework. Since teachers now have a looming fear of being marked down for not engaging in constant instruction, students miss these opportunities to communicate and they themselves have heightened anxiety.

Often when I have asked someone older that appears happy in their career why they decided to go into that field, I hear "I had a teacher in high school tell me I would be good at it." A conversation with a teacher fostered a career. Currently there are so many students in a classroom, teachers barely know their students so these types of conversations are not happening as often.

Teachers also feel the encumbrance of delivering long lectures which is another reason students lose interest and zone out. Information needs to be brief, to the point, interesting, and engaging. When students are already inattentive and they are being thrust into rigorous classes, their motivation can be compromised. Now imagine these same students being thrown into advanced classes. Oh my, what a disaster.

For some kids, the regular curriculum is demanding enough to prepare for post high school. It would benefit students greatly to look at college websites and see what high school courses are needed for admittance. Many students just by being involved in a regular curriculum have far exceeded expectations. Students should also keep in mind that out of state colleges could have different criteria as well. For example, the University of Alabama only requires 1 year of a foreign language.

Self-fulfillment is about hard work, altruism, and the ability to connect to mankind. Kids are shutting down because they do not understand the convoluted process of transitioning from high school to college, relationships with educated professional is amiss, and interactions with peers is scarce. To acquire and retain student success there needs to be more teacher interaction and less technology. A computer doesn't ask a student how they are doing, what they did over the weekend, what they need help with, and how things are at home. The care and compassion that is evident in a teacher's demeanor can mean the world to a young adult.

Education is about the relationships, the people, and the connections. Kids need to know they are not on an island alone. It is important to understand they need to stand by one another, which entails relying on others. This is why treating peers kindly is vital to success. Intrapersonal skills aid in performance. It is difficult, however, to expect students to have intrapersonal communication with one another when staff is unable to model this behavior.

Take Starbucks for example, while every other coffee company is closing, Starbucks continues to expand. The difference is the personal attention given to costumers. When someone orders a coffee, they are asked their name. The worker then puts the person's name on the cup and when the drink order is ready, the person is called by their name. Not a number, but their actual name. This simple tactic has made people feel special thus causing them to return. They are even willing to pay more than the average cup of java costs. They are paying for that personal recognition; the company identifying how significant this human sentiment is has led to huge profits.

Social media has led to a society of impatient people that want immediate responses. When responses are not given in a timely fashion, people freak out. While society needs to learn to be more patient, organizations need to understand people should be serviced and if this means hiring more staff, then it should be done.

Student Capital

I recall a conversation with an administrator where I exclaimed 461 students is too many, and with the increase in paperwork it is impossible to service them in the way they need to be serviced. The response, "yeah, we are all doing more with less, I understand." That reply is a validation of the problem, but not a solution.

Suicide, depression, addiction, anxiety, and bullying being on the rise correlates with the challenge of connecting with students, improper delivery of information, and a rise in teacher burn out. In the midst of all this, in many districts central office personnel are highly compensated. Rather than figure these issues out; actions such as robbing from Peter to pay Paul create larger gaps. When looking at the distribution of funds, perhaps management of money is a bigger problem in education than one might realize.

Since students are lacking guidance, personal connections, and the fundamentals of reading, writing, math, science, and social studies; they need to step up and start helping themselves. Students need to start conquering some of the fears they have or they will fall behind their peers, way behind. Nothing makes a person happier than doing well on a tough job. Success is not instant and that is part of the problem. Everyone wants to start at the top of the ladder instead of at the bottom and move up. This sense of needing immediate gratification leads to disappointment.

People become bored with jobs that have confined hours, but the truth is people need to learn how to work within the constraints of confinement. By doing so, perhaps they won't mistake the inability to complete a task as a mental illness. Instead, they will persevere and learn how to master that skill, which can be easily accomplished with repetition. They will also learn to have self-respect, dress and act appropriately, and acquire a sense of privacy. Knowing how to filter what they share about their life is important too so they don't later have a repository of guilt for sharing too much.

Tips for students on relaxation:

Find what makes you feel good

When you feel good, you relax

When you relax, you think

When you think, you create

Students need techniques to help put their mind at ease. Their brains are over stimulated and they need to be able to focus. Breathing exercises, stress toys, fresh air, and laughter all help rejuvenate the senses so mindfulness can be present. Students have reported the more stress they are under, the more difficult it is to recall information and perform tasks. Students usually don't deny that they should relax more but not knowing how to accomplish relaxation is a huge disconnect. The why and how cavity is expanding among millennials and instead of inquiring how to do something, they silently suffer.

Student Capital in Higher Education

Through the years students and parents alike have commented on the college application process noting, "I have done everything right and it still didn't work." Of course, they are not taking into consideration the system is flawed whereas the odds were never in their favor. Being part of a flawed system sometimes is difficult to realize and even more difficult to come to terms with. As a high school guidance counselor there is a wealth of knowledge I should be sharing with families and can't due to mundane tasks now being asked of me. Schools believe they have done their due diligence because students are referred to a one-stop shop for information online.

Putting that mindset in perspective, schools are willing to invest time and money into a software program but not into personal guidance. Unfortunately, no one is showing students and parents how to utilize such sites. When someone takes the time to sit down and show someone how to do something it helps the other person see the value in what they are doing. The process of offering a handout with instructions on how to complete a task may seem helpful, but does not allow for questions and answers.

This is where once again activity becomes confused with achievement. A person being re-directed to a computer site or piece of literature does not offer the guidance needed to acquire success. Each student is different, therefore so are their needs. Technology should be used as an aid, not a replacement. Using it to replace individual care is confusing, misleading, and disastrous to say the least.

Students come to higher education institutions not knowing how to learn because they have not mastered the task of hard work and effort. For example, students are more inclined to take pictures of notes than write them down which is one reason they don't remember much. For the most part, they are not really interested in the subject, so true learning does not actually take place because the student doesn't care if they actually know the material or not, they only care about the grade.

However, exposing students to various degree paths could spark that interest. Once that interest is initiated, further exploration can lend to learning about jobs in that career path and when the student connects the job with the education, learning will take on a whole new meaning. Most importantly, selecting a degree path that is marketable will inspire a student to complete the program and start earning an income.

I often wonder why colleges have such generic degree programs that a student can do absolutely nothing with. For example, health sciences, what does that even mean? It is so broad of a topic and denotes such a large array of disciplines many students have a difficult time utilizing it. Universities need to stop leading kids down a narrow pathway where the only option they have after graduation is to keep paying and keep going to school.

Higher education institutions should hire more college counselors to better serve and guide these students on what programs exist, what careers can be derived from those programs, and what courses should be taken. The present system has left kids clueless, disengaged and frustrated. Furthermore, offering kids a personality test and learning styles test may offer insight to who they are. This insight can help guide their learning.

Post-secondary education needs to start servicing students better or they are going to decline in enrollment. Take Dick's Sporting Goods as an example, while numerous franchises and stores are closing, Dick's is expanding opening bigger stores and more of them. Can anyone guess why in an economy where online shopping has overruled store shopping this company would take such a high risk in growing its franchise? Anyone that knows anything about business wouldn't be a bit surprised because Dick's has amazing customer service. They are well staffed, friendly, helpful, knowledgeable about the merchandise, and always look for ways for a customer to save money.

Compare this to Dunham's where no one is ever on the floor to assist customers, hardly any registers are opened, and they could care less if you save money or not. While one industry is booming, another is nearly bankrupt. Blame it on hard economic times all you want, I believe customer service directly impacts the success and failure of these companies. Investing in employees is investing in the company because those employees are front and center. Similarly, investing in students is investing in our nation because these students are the future.

Higher Education institutions need to start investing in student capital by closing the gap of what students know and what students need to know. Meanwhile, student needs to empower themselves. This can be accomplished by asking questions, seeking opportunities, and networking. College students need to get connected and stay involved. Since a vast majority of high school training is not adequate to sustain learning in college, students need to learn how to study, take notes, and review material. This can help alleviate the influx of students needing remediation at the college level; hence spending more time and money on their education.

This is partially due to not being properly educated and just being passed through the broken system, but it is also due to lack of accountability on the students' part. Rather than manipulating the system students need to embrace instruction and truly benefit from it. The only way a student is going to do that is by completing the work; if they are not working then they are not learning. Even attentive listening is working the mind.

I don't know anyone that has ever accomplished anything by not having to work at it. Yet, that is the unrealistic view that has been established for these millenniums. Even parents allow kids to stay home and not go to school. When students don't come to school and no one at the school handles truancy, parents are left exasperated and more pressure is placed on the teacher to make sure students perform; the student has just received a get out of jail free card because no one blames them for their lack of effort.

Stop, slow down, and let's think about this. A child has the option to tell their parents they are not going to school? A parent has no control over this? A teacher is responsible for a kid that never attends school? A school has no consequence for a child not coming to school? How is that even realistic? That is just plain ridiculous, so the teacher just passes the student and everyone is happy. Until everyone realizes the student hasn't learned a thing. Now fast forward to the college level, a student misses class, the instructor doesn't "just pass him or her through" and that student has a complete meltdown. The student doesn't have the foundation from high school and is struggling at the college level. What a mess!

If a student is not mature enough to attend college, then they shouldn't. There is no law that states this is the path a person has to take. Not everyone is college bound and some people simply need more time to figure life out. Post high school is not a race to see who can graduate first. Rather, the only race a person has to engage in is against him or herself. No one else really matters. Everyone seems to be just going through the motions. When people rush, they make errors. People need to stop, slow down, and do things right. Even if a student does earn a degree, if they did not learn the information they are bringing less value to the workplace. This too has become a mounting concern.

The lack of skills students have to function at a job has become alarming. Not only are skills remiss, so too are ethics and values in the workplace. Just like some students are not dedicated to their learning, these same students are not dedicated to their employer. Too many young adults do not know how to perform simple functions like laundry, dishes, packing a lunch, or yard work. The reason they don't know how is because they have never had to do it; someone else always did it for them. Some high school aged students still have parents that pack their lunch for them and even go as far as to make them breakfast too. This type of child has an extremely difficult time assimilating to college, work, or society in general.

Student Capital

Ever since a student was little, they were taught to pick a career path, a career goal, and to figure out what they want to do in life. I am now hearing legislation asserts career education needs to be pushed down to lower elementary. Wow, are they really that clueless? If a 17 year old high school student is not mature enough to process what is involved in a profession why would anyone think a 7 year old can? Children can experience occupations without having to pick just one. If the process of exposing kids to various areas of future livelihood is not implemented correctly, kids will stress out and shut down.

Look at all the homework elementary kids get and the enormous amount of stress they have and this is only elementary school. I am beside myself when I hear of elementary level kids being on depression and/or anxiety medication. There are better ways to manage stress. There are also ways to alleviate stress.

Don't think for a second the elementary level kids are immune to cheating- just look through their phones. Since too much information is state mandated and it is almost impossible to cover all of it in a given school year, material is rushed through which leads to low test scores; however, many elementary level kids are often permitted to retest to raise their grade. Yes, that is correct, take the test over again. Nevertheless, the grade a parent sees may not have been the student's first attempt. College does not permit retesting; so at a young age children are being set up for future failure.

That is to say they are being conditioned to think this is how school should be. Indeed, in actuality if students are given less information to remember they would do a much better job recalling it. To illustrate this point, students test scores would more than likely increase by giving student's 4 exams with 15 questions on each exam as opposed to one exam with 60 questions. The same material is being covered, except it is broken down into smaller parts.

It is very difficult to get students interested in a career program when they are not even coming to school. All the same, students that do express interest in a particular field should explore that area more; even independently. One way to do this is to contact people in the field and understand more about the occupation, job growth, pay, and hiring practices. For example, if someone indicates they want to be a dental hygienist, they can contact local dentists, possibly job shadow, inquire which school they prefer to hire from and why.

This information can prove useful in determining if this career is right for them. It also can help them understand why they need to take certain classes and how the information learned will be applied in the field. When students understand why they are doing something, they are more likely to care about how to do it.

I recall when selecting a topic for my dissertation my committee kept asking, "So what" and "Why is this important." They kept asking me this so as to emphasize what I was doing had meaning. Once I understood the why, I had to determine the how; meaning what was I going to do to accomplish this goal. Connecting the two was the key to completing my dissertation.

I heard a startling statistic that 50% of students are not graduating from college. I also heard this statistics is only based on students that start as a freshman and transfer students are not part of the equation; which makes one wonder if transfer students are more successful. A lot of higher education institutions are doling out money to try to figure out what the problem is with retention, but not as much of a commitment is being placed upon implementing change. Surveys are not asking students the right questions. Students are choosing colleges based on affordability, not choice. The students more than likely not graduating haven't learned how to learn. Keep in mind a high school transcript should no longer be used as an indicator of success.

If more colleges were within a student's means, students would be more likely to attend a college that had a program they were interested in. What is happening instead, they are going to colleges that are less expensive and in this process limiting their choices. Once at a college that perhaps wasn't by choice, students feel forced to select a curriculum and sometimes pick one that doesn't really appeal to them. By doing so, they are less likely to complete it.

Once again, colleges need to offer better advising for students. They need to seek students out and build relationships with them so they feel comfortable inquiring about things they don't understand. Students need mentors that can guide them in how to be a college student until they become familiar with the process.

Investing in these types of employees is better use of finances. College is a business that services students, therefore colleges need to invest in the quality of service being offered. Furthermore, the more goal oriented a student is, the less likely they will be to **abuse substances**. Students have reported using drugs for 3 main reasons:

1. They are bored.
2. They are stressed.
3. They lack a sense of belonging.

Having something of interest to focus on can alleviate these factors. Such a simple concept, yet constantly overlooked.

Colleges need to find a better practice for connecting with students because what is currently in place does not appear to be working. Students feel misled sometimes once they start attending college. This is because the recruiter was so attentive while trying to get a student to sign with a particular college, but once there, no one seems to care about them. This becomes a devastating discovery.

I understand colleges have people in place to meet with students, but do those people actually spend time getting to know the student? If I had to guess, I would say "no" because getting to know someone takes a lot of time, and students have gone away to college and come back only to say they feel "rushed", "disregarded," and "insignificant," when talking to a professor or advisor. Then I remind them they are paying to feel that way; which almost embarrasses them.

Being connected helps when deciding on a career path. When I was working on my doctorate in college I knew I had a professor I could turn to and ask just about anything. Even when this professor left the college to go to a different college, he still continued to mentor me, which meant a lot. There were times I was frustrated, self-doubting, and burnt out and he always helped me to put things back in perspective. This is the type of relationship needed when selecting a field to study.

Career paths like business, science, math, and engineering are very narrow and can cause students not to understand what these fields necessitate. Knowing what types of jobs relate to these career paths could help a student decide what they want to major in. There are so many options available which students do not fathom.

As previously mentioned, what would help is if students took a learning style inventory and a personality test. The way a person acquires knowledge coupled with their disposition could better align with their interest. Students take interest inventories and they seem to be meaningless without knowing their personality type and learning style. The three go hand-in-hand when determining the best fit for a career. A reform in education should incorporate all three tests being taken. The students I have had complete these seem to become more serious about their education because they understand more about whom they are and the modality in which they learn.

Finding out one's learning style is critical because once they discover how they learn; they can better prepare to learn. I have asked numerous college reps what students should do to prepare for college and many proclaim, "Fill their toolbox with as much as possible." This is because students need to be equipped with a desire to learn, quest to do better and interest in being a self-sustaining human being continually striving for excellence. Most importantly, today's youth need to learn how to communicate. How does this spike in social anxiety fit into this structure? It doesn't.

I ask because when accommodations are given to students at the high school level, it is not a realistic reflection of societal norms; the college can't make people go away and if a student is unable to do a fundamental part of their work due to intense uneasiness of being around others, perhaps a college environment is not for them.

The doctors that write scripts allowing kids to avoid social situations rather than conquer them, and the parents that enable their student by insisting these avoidance measures are enforced, and the school systems that are too afraid to take a stand- have all led kids down a path of unrealistic events. If a student's academic performance on their transcript is not a true reflection of what they know, that student will inevitably struggle at the college level.

Accommodations in high schools have become the majority rather than the minority; which is very troubling. Furthermore, these accommodations are about making the student happy, when they should be about healing. Restorative measures include awareness of one's own self-destruction or thinking trap; none of which ever gets addressed. This could be why anxiety increases instead of decreasing. If a student is disillusioned into thinking others can "fix" their anxious state of mind, then they will not work at finding change. Without change, the problem will continue to exist.

Showing care and concern from the college goes a long way too. A student once told me he decided on which college to attend by the lunch lady. I asked him to elaborate on that and he explained, "when I visited this particular college, we were given lunch in the school cafeteria. The lunch lady behind the counter started asking me questions like what major I might pursue and where I was from, I thought gosh, if she cares this much everyone must." Impressions are important in everything we do and sometimes people are forgetful of that.

I know I used a similar concept when seeking a doctor; if the receptionist was nice and friendly I found out more about the practice, if I was given rude or insincere acknowledgement, I didn't waste my time with that particular office. Of course, I never thought the same concept would apply to young adults, but after talking with this student I totally realize it does. And it totally makes sense.

Interestingly, the people you don't expect to notice you do and when this happens it says a lot about the establishment. Being a person, rather than a number, is so important. This goes back to making personal connections; which inspires students to work hard and be all encompassing. I actually had a college representative tell me once that she switched from a large school to a smaller one because at the larger school none of the professors knew her name. This caused her to feel disconnected. Rather than quit college altogether, she found a setting that better suited her needs. Finding what works, through trial and error, is all part of maturity, growth, and building character.

The most successful students learn to advocate on their own behalf. They know how to navigate a college campus, and understand how to manage their time. Learning takes place when a student is challenged. Students need to ask for help, so communication skills are essential. Resources are available, but many students do not make an effort to seek these means out. Students are not critical thinkers; rather they just want the answer.

This type of conditioning has been a detriment to their learning. By not paying attention to detail, they can easily be taken advantage of. A spike in tuition is one example. One college every year went up by $100 a credit hour. Students got the answer, which is how much they owed, but they didn't arrive at the conclusion of why that was how much they owed, so they were oblivious to the tuition increases. Students need to be cautious of this trend. Once they are so many credit hours into the program, they have no choice but to pay the increased fee so they can complete their degree. The feeling of being stuck is not a good feeling.

Colleges have a lot of damage control since students come from a culture of excessive testing and cheating. Sadly, more attention in the school systems is focused on ensuring reliable (yield the same results with multiple trials) and valid (measures what it is supposed to) data, then helping kids understand what a primary class is. While technology is advancing and platforms are being created for students to submit online portfolios listing achievements from 9th grade on, student skill sets are declining and they continue to struggle with basic fundamental principles like what constitutes a core class and the relevance in taking one.

The concept of online portfolios is such that admission advisors can take a look at these portfolios and determine admissions or help guide students since many schools are not well staffed with guidance counselors to aid in the application process. This is a horrible solution because kids are not mature, do not have a relationship with college representatives, and usually do not have a clue what they want to do. Strategies of this nature are hollow. In the end, like everything else, students just go through the motions with little to no meaning.

I fear getting kids where they want to be instead of where they need to be. A student may be able to create the most elaborate portfolio, yet still not realize foreign languages are considered core classes. Everyone is so focused on digital learning, real learning is becoming non-existent. Unless the student plans on majoring in industrial technology, critical components of academia are missing with technology based learning.

If you think I am wrong, ask a teen what core academic classes are and watch them stutter as they answer. Then ask them to create a video with edits and sound and you will be amazed. If that is alright because technology is so highly valued, then stop complaining that kids don't know anything. Everyone keeps feeding into kids not knowing anything then acts shocked when exposed.

It can't be both ways; if colleges want students to have basic knowledge then stop asking for such high tech processes. Education is about relationships. The reason some online programs work is because of the connection, not the instruction. The computer itself isn't inspiring the student to do the work, but the coach, tutor, email, and text reminders are.

You Don't Know What You Don't Ask

Students need to understand the only person in charge of their learning is themselves. The education students receive lies within their boundaries. The biggest mistake a student can make in college is relying solely on others to impart great wisdom upon them. The instructors' role is to guide learning, not create it. Generating knowledge is the responsibility of the student and the wisdom gained is reflective of how much effort a student is willing to put forth.

While the American kids appear to be in crisis, there is still hope for future generations to fulfill the American Dream and a good way to accomplish that is to understand that where one starts may not be where one ends up and there is absolutely nothing wrong with that. Paths change, things happen, and life takes its toll; but the ability to persevere is created within the individual, not something that is sold or handed to them.

This is why "safe zones" have come into play on college campuses, student are incapable of handling matters that pertain to uncertainty. While I agree this past election was different than most elections, the mere fact that a college aged student is unable to function because of not being able to process the election results and has to go to a designated place to work through these feelings and emotions is concerning. Working through these emotions with others is fine; the inability to perform daily tasks because of concerns over who got elected president is somewhat extreme.

All areas of a college campus should be considered nonviolent, peaceful, and inviting; if they are not, delegating one area is not going to cut it. Furthermore, if a conversation or movement takes place that is uncomfortable for a person, that person needs to figure out why and deal with it. Disengaging only makes them less informed, and draws more attention to a person; which sometimes is the real goal.

College aged students need to be better informed on worldly issues. The sad, unfortunate truth is people love to take advantage of other people. Numerous businesses have become deceiving, misleading, sneaky, and most of all greedy. However, it is somewhat the consumers fault as well. Your financial loss is someone else's gain. Patrons need to protect what is rightfully theirs and the best way to accomplish this is by asking questions; lots of questions.

Don't be so quick to give away your hard earned cash. Read the fine print, expirations, and exclusions on forms. Ask for a summary of charges when placing special orders. There are a lot of extra's added on that a person doesn't need and you are not told of different options because you didn't ask. Look up reviews on products; know stipulations of dates on receipts for returns, and check termination conditions for contracts. Taking cautious measures can help avoid being scammed.

Since there are so many budget cuts in industries employees sometimes hold multiple jobs making it difficult to dedicate time to reviewing pertinent documents. Focusing on servicing the customer has become less of a priority and finding the quickest, most manipulative way to make money has become the focal point of many companies. This is even more of a reason why the consumer has to look out for himself.

Think about coupons for a second. These are usually mailed, emailed, or even texted to people. Once you go into the store or fill your shopping cart online, you realize it can only be used on certain days, for certain items (usually never anything on sale) at certain locations. Since you are at checkout, you don't want to be bothered, so you just buy the damn thing without the coupon that brought you into the store or to the site to begin with.

People then tend to feel buyer's remorse because they bought something they didn't really need, but thought they could justify the purchase because they would be getting a deal on it. Some places are fabulous and will give you the discount anyway; most places could care less if you put everything down and walk out. It is not the establishment itself that is unconcerned; it is the employee who lacks decent pay and proper training. One way to avoid this pitfall is when entering a store, immediately find a sales clerk and inquire on what you can and can't use your coupon on. If no employee is in sight, or unsure themselves, that is a sign that you will not be getting the biggest bang for your buck and before investing your time looking at merchandise, you may want to do yourself a favor and walk out. You will feel more in control of your spending and less frustrated with devious marketing techniques.

Special orders are the biggest culprit of scheming. I have noticed like college tuition, many stores do not offer an itemized break down of what things cost; they just give a bottom dollar. This tacit makes the consumer feel as though there are no other options, which usually is not true. My daughter and I once went to a store because we wanted to custom frame a picture she had painted with her now deceased aunt. Since her aunt was no longer alive this picture was very meaningful. We went to this particular store because we had a 70% off custom framing coupon. The clerk informed us for the 8 x 10 portrait it would cost $186.33. We presented her the coupon and she exclaimed "oh, I already took that off."

Being caught up in our emotions of the painting, we almost paid it; but then decided to ask questions. This was when we identified all the extras that were added on that we didn't indicate we wanted. Such embellishments included double border, upgraded frame, and top of the line glass with scratch resistant and anti-glare. We weren't hanging this in a museum, but in our home for our very own eyes. After we vetoed most of the additions, we ended up paying $55.90 for the picture and it looked great.

One of the reasons we thought to ask questions is because we almost got scammed in this same manner at the eye doctor. We were given a bottom dollar without a break down and when we asked for an itemized list we quickly realized we did not need all the extras or upgrades. We knocked our bill in half. Think of all the people that are so aggravated they just pay it. Or they don't inquire because they don't want to appear frugal.

When you are paying for a product or service you have every right to request more information. Just because a person appears nice doesn't mean they are honest. Some of the nicest people are the biggest con-artists because you wouldn't suspect they are capable of such foul play. Young adults don't always realize the capacity of scams and can become easy targets.

CHAPTER 9
TECHNOLOGY ADDICTION DISORDER

"It's not a faith in technology.
It's faith in people."

~Steve Jobs

Technology Abuse

Students are disconnected with school and it is causing a debacle in education. Politicians assert American children are behind in learning. The resolution; have a more stringent curriculum. If America is indeed behind in learning, it is not due to a lack of rigor. Kids of today's generation are very smart and have a lot of potential; it just isn't channeled properly.

They are amazing at manipulating technology. They make videos with subtitles and graphics and pose with confidence when taking pictures. They multi-task various social media sites using numerous electronic devices and download games for leisure. They have learned how to configure and reconfigure systems. In fact, they have even figured out how to create virtual sites for school work which enable them to share answers. This gesture personifies them as young adults engaged in academics when they actually are not; which is quite devious.

Students are so good at utilizing technology, schools have embraced it. The problem is technology in and of itself is not enough to sustain what a student needs to know in life. Instead of teaching them what they don't know, schools offer more of what they are already good at. Since students are masters of technology, they don't use it for learning; they use it to get around learning. They search answers to math equations, copy essays, skim reviews on literary reading, and get answers to science experiments they never conducted.

They have no clue how to calculate the answer for a math problem, or how to write an essay using their own thoughts and proper grammar, the importance of literature or even the value in exploration and problem solving. They have answers by technological resources and that is all they have. Yet, they give the impression that they know how to derive the answer and in their world that is good enough.

Once students step outside their world to college or the workforce the masquerade becomes too hard to keep up, which is why so many kids are plummeting. This is because not every student is college bound and forcing kids to take classes that are too difficult is only going to shut them down or cause them to scam. Even at the college level, students are manipulating learning by paying someone to do their work, bypassing software to configure the answers, or copying work from peers or the internet. I am amazed at the multiple ways students cheat. Surely cheating has been around for decades, nonetheless a preponderance of students are cheating at the college level no doubt causing distress when entering the work place and perhaps need to use skills they should have learned in college, but bypassed.

Although it would be easy for society to blame electronics and social media for the problems youths are having, this aspect is a small portion of a bigger issue. Electronics in and of itself is not the issue; rather it is the accessibility and obsession with these devices that causes concern. Creativity once emerged from a child not having anything to do. Now that void is filled with a virtual world where many parents are not mindful of what sites or apps their child is engaged in and some of these sites promote risky behavior. Parents themselves are guilty of overindulgence in social media thus neglecting their child's needs.

One of the key elements to raising a healthy, normal child is to be part of his or her life so when transitions exist or curiosities arise, kids aren't turning to the internet for answers. Granted, many teens are not intellectually mature enough to determine propaganda from truth. While a youth's ability to engage in numerous aspects of technology is fascinating, it is also consuming.

For one thing, many teens have become so addicted to gaming that it interferes with the daily functioning of their life. Some adolescents and adults have become such competitive gamers they steal money, disappear for days on end, and make excuses not to attend school or family events so they can game. They feel guilty for being involved in such disruptive behavior, so they attempt to change, experience withdraws, and find ways to nurture the habit like skipping class and hiding in the restroom or holing up in their bedroom. They become very angry individuals because they do not know how to admit they have a problem. Therefore, they shift the blame on everyone and everything else. Yet addictive behavior is addictive behavior and unless it is addressed, it will continue to disrupt their life and the lives of everyone around them.

When people are engorged in electronics all day, little else is accomplished and then they feel remorseful for not accomplishing anything. Instead of owning up to the fact that their behavior significantly contributed to their emotional state, they instead opt towards self-pity, multiple excuses, and manipulation. Whether people consciously or unconsciously realize this is what is happening, others feed into it allowing this mannerism to exist and continue.

Young adults do not choose to be motivated, useful, or have a positive self-image because they do not have to; everyone accepts, even praises them, for being just the way they are, no matter how nefarious it may seem.

The electronics become addicting and people accept these habits as the way of the world. It doesn't have to be and shouldn't be and obsessions with these devices are ruining our youth. So many other skills and talents can be harvested if kids weren't so occupied all the time with electronics.

That is to say if you had all day to do nothing but master technology, you too would be an expert. So really kids aren't doing anything remarkable. Quite frankly, they should be able to operate various facets of technology because they are on it constantly. Anything a person engages in continuously they will incidentally become better at. Kids, tweens, teens, and even some adults exert so much energy on technological devices they do not have much vitality for anything else.

Electronics have consumed every aspect of their lives. The problem with this is the people that complain about kids spending so much time on devices are the same people that bought those devices for those kids. What did you expect to happen? Kids have become so obsessed with social media, apps, and games that they use those same electronic devices to manipulate learning so they can get back to their virtual world. They are consumed, obsessed, and addicted to these devices and it is the adults that encourage this behavior. Everyone thinks kids aren't learning because they are distracted with electronics, while that may play a role, the even bigger picture is they are not doing their work; they are cheating, finding shortcuts, and not putting forth the time and effort to actually learn the material. The American people are facing an erudition crisis because no one is willing to accept blame or admit fault. Everyone points the finger, accuses others, feels victimized, and expects someone else to fix the problem.

A huge decision a person can make that will significantly impact their life is to put away electronics. That's right, completely out of sight. These devices have become such a big distraction that people are sidetracked from living life. Electronics have overpowered peoples sleep, learning, bonding, communicating, and existence in real time. It has interrupted precious periods with loved ones, overshadowed special moments, and thwarted peoples focus.

First, more accidents and deaths have occurred with using electronics while driving. Second, less learning is taking place and third, verbal communication has become awkward. In the same fashion, a lot of energy is being put into taking the perfect selfie and less emphasis is being placed on understanding the fundamentals of arithmetic and proper grammar.

To further exasperate this abuse of technology, young drivers lack a sense of direction because as passengers they are on their electronic devices instead of paying attention to road signs and familiar surroundings. Parents, rather than having eloquent conversations with their kids, follow them on social media in hopes of getting a glimpse of what is going on in their life. Parents spend an ornate amount of time at events and functions trying to capture the perfect picture or video so they can share it with others and get a large percentage of "likes."

Seldom does the parent ever watch the video or view that picture again yet they spent so much time trying to capture the moment, they actually miss the moment seeing it through the lens of a device rather than with their very own eyes. No one really remembers a picture taken and posted; but people often remember things they see first-hand. Put away the devices, watch with your eyes, feel with your heart, remember with your mind, and pay attention. Life is a series of memories and electronics are robbing people from creating fond memoirs.

Inept Communication Whilst Embracing Technology

Students need to know how to think and reason on a higher level for any career field. As the Baby Boomer generation begins to retire from critical skill-based jobs and trades, others will be needed to fill those positions. However, where society is falling short is in teaching this younger generation how to communicate, about different cultures, learning empathy, and gaining insight on how people think.

These all-encompassing skills will not only make well-rounded students and employees, but will help to create a better society. This is accomplished if the true goal of higher learning is to educate people, young and old, to think and act on a higher level of intelligence and consciousness, along with using that knowledge to help society.

One of the reasons teens are so irascible is because of their inability to communicate. By not flexing communication skills, they are limiting their potential to get out into the public, which in turn hinders opportunity. Being honest and reflective of one's skills and aware of what retooling is necessary is essential to stay employable in a changing world. Selecting a career field can be a daunting task, which is why the process should be broken down into smaller parts focusing on skill sets such as communicating, decision-making, and self-discovery. Through these modes a person can better assess career options.

Many school systems are promoting the digital age; which embraces technology and cell phone use, hence causing a bigger issue. I am stunned at what an integral role technology plays in education. Not only are teachers creating websites and online learning tools to assist students; they are also using email, texting, and various apps to support learning. It sounds great in theory, but in reality is totally confusing.

Teachers are expected to use different teaching methods to reach their students individualized learning needs. To justify use of these high tech expensive programs, teachers redirect students to them. Students want an answer not an app. So, the student begrudgingly downloads whatever it is they need, completes it haphazardly, and turns it in to receive credit. No true learning took place.

People think because students are tech savvy with some things they are with everything which is foolish thinking. Kids are good with their phones, videos, and various apps because they are interested in those options and outcomes; so they will choose to spend hours experimenting with these software programs. If they would dedicate the same amount of time prepping for a test, they would do well on it, but they don't because the material is not interesting, they see no value in it, and no one answers their questions.

If kids knew how to study they may have a greater appreciation of knowledge. No one takes the time to show them, like everything else, they expect kids to just know how to partake in this process. Since kids of today lack communication skills, they don't ask. Perhaps schools should give less homework and spend more time teaching the value of learning.

Another emerging concern with technology is students don't know what to do with information they find on the internet. When battling puberty or other important phases of life, kids are resorting to opinionated links that could misguide them. Often they struggle with information they find and don't know where to direct questions or who to trust.

Having a knowledgeable experienced person to converse with would avoid randomly asking the internet; above all, the internet has been known to lead to cyber bullying. This is because platforms exist like "ask. fm," a social networking site where questions are asked about others, or "high school polls," where students post questions about other kids with a yes or no answer and other students vote on it, then the next day the results are listed. A question might be "is Jane Doe an undercover slut?" Sometimes the question is a comparison like "who is better at basketball Kid X or Helen Keller?" Such questions are cruel, insensitive, and offensive and teens have expressed fear, agitation, and hurt over such deliberate attacks.

As a result of such unkind remarks, they spend hours wondering who could be so insulting or worry peers might think the question posted is true. Their confidence, self-esteem, and ability to focus are compromised and they are left with a pit in their stomach that begins to interfere with daily functioning. They are too embarrassed or ashamed to seek guidance so they suffer silently until they get to a breaking point and possibly harm themselves or another. Often, parents and educators aren't even aware the situation exists.

Social media has become problematic in other ways as well, such as suicidal tendencies. Kids post a plan to kill themselves and peers "like" it or try to counsel the individual. However, such peers are not professionals and comments or suggestions made, in response to a person's desperation, becomes perplexing. When a person is at a point in their life where they want to end it, they are experiencing an increase in agony that they do not know how to handle. Usually, this individual does not want to die, they just want to get rid of the horrific emotional pain they are feeling and lack the necessary skills to cope with it. The most important aspect of coping is compassion and sometimes peers do not know how to accurately express empathy.

When a person commits suicide, they are completing a frantic last act because they are consumed by so much psychological pain they think it is the only way out and truly believe they are doing others around them a favor. Peers do not realize the risk factors involved when a person feels worthless and therefore should be better informed on what to do when someone they know creates a hopeless post and shares it with others.

Educating youths on signs of helplessness and whom to contact could prevent potential deaths. More education is needed in this realm and more staff should be available for students to have personal connections with. **This is the key to suicide prevention**. A relationship entails talking and getting to know someone over time, not an outsourced staff member that periodically checks in or receives very little pay and benefits and is bitter towards the employer.

Today's youths often use social media to validate themselves, when in truth; social media is who they want to be, not who they are. The problem is they spend so much time on these electronic devices they live a hermetic life, which is extremely unhealthy. Parents need to create a culture in their home that reinforces boundaries and limits on these devices.

Regrettably, electronic communication has become their main method of socializing, but what they are not being taught is how to receive and decode messages. Due to their lack of non-verbal communication the true meaning of a message gets lost and is not interpreted the way the sender intended. Miscommunication has become a common occurrence in this digital age.

Talking to young adults about the relevance of online communication and the proper way to disseminate online messages can prevent abuse or misuse of the tool. Agreeably, having them practice face-to-face communication can also lessen being misunderstood.

Educating parents may be necessary as well. However, this may take a lot of convincing because like most things society does not want to admit an issue exists. Parents know their child is engaged in unhealthy behaviors with technological devices, but consider it ok because all kids of this generation are. On the contrary, just because everyone is doing something that doesn't make the act any healthier. Turning a blind eye to something so significantly damaging will yield disastrous results.

For example, due to the decreased level of face-to-face communications and increase in online communications, students are not able to form friendships and bonds with their peers like former generations did. The inability to form deep emotional connections with others impacts their emotional health. Less connections with friends equates to less support when having to deal with life issues. By not having a support system in place self-esteem is impacted because a person starts questioning themselves and has no one to confirm or deny behaviors and thoughts.

Dr. Krolczyk

In a recent conversation with another parent, it was casually mentioned that her 4th grader is up until 6:00 a.m. watching Netflix, then sleeps the next day until 2:00 or 3:00 in the afternoon. She suggested this was a regular occurrence and at least her 8th grader was better; he only stays up until 3:00 a.m. playing Xbox. This parent also explained that when she tried to restrict their access to these devices her children actually displayed withdrawal symptoms such as tremors, and anxiousness. The addictions kids have with these devices are alarming because in the real world, essentially the workplace, the inability to perform duties and tasks due to sleep deprivation can result in job loss.

If young adults were to actually journal the amount of time they spend on these electronic devices they would be shocked. Once again, where schools fall short is in bringing awareness to this issue. The epidemic of over usage of electronic devices has become as big of an impact on human growth and development as substance abuse and bullying.

Kids usual turn to self-destructive behaviors when they are bored. For example, I had a student that was a habitual shoplifter. She came from a family that provided above and beyond her needs. When I asked her why she continues to shoplift, when she doesn't need to, her response was, "because I am bored, my parents drop me off at the mall for like 4 hours and I run out of things to do." Since kids have nothing else to do, they succumb to these devices- which in time turns into an addiction. It saddens me how little children play with one another.

Part of the problem with inept communication is students do not know how to express themselves; so they resort to arguing. For instance, a colleague of mine at the college told a story about a student that started arguing with him when he was in the middle of a lecture because the student did not agree with the date the exam was scheduled for. As if that was not un-couth enough, after class, the student defended her actions by stating that her tuition paid the professors salary so she and her classmates should determine the structure of the class. This absurd sense of entitlement is causing major issues for people.

Consequently, the student ended up dropping the course, but not before writing a complaint to the dean blaming the professor for her poor performance. It was much more feasible in this student's mind to hold the professor liable for her lack of success than to admit poor study habits and lack of time management contributing to her overall grade. While she did petition other students to agree with her outlandish accusations, none of them went as far to jeopardize their grade. This student was very foolish in the sense that while she thought she was rallying against a professor, in the end she was the only one that suffered negative consequences as a result of her actions.

CHAPTER 10

SUCCESS IS POSSIBLE

"Sometimes we need to accept we are only capable of doing so much at one time"

~Dr. Krolczyk

Finding Solutions

In view of the aforementioned, a troubled society exists. There can be numerous contributing factors, but in the end these are only descriptions and not solutions. When looking at the educational infrastructure, perhaps legislators feel teachers are overpaid, have an easy job, or too much time off.

A government official may view the teacher as the bad guy, but what they neglect to realize is abusing teachers has a direct impact on kids and it is not the terrible teacher that is the problem, but the oppressed system. Unless of course it is a conspiracy theory and government officials are intentionally ruining school systems so as to benefit politically and financially from charter, private and online schools.

This is a horrible accusation and if there is even a remote possibility that such a theory is true, the American educational system will never be great again. People are wasting their efforts fighting a cause that will never be won. Federal and state regimes need to work with districts, not against them.

Administrators need to work with teachers, not against them. Finally, parents need to work with schools, not against them. Every member of a team needs to be considered a valuable asset for the team to function at its best and obtain its goal of maximizing student capital™; seeing that today's students are tomorrow's future. Teachers are terribly under paid, and teaching has become a profession no one wants to go into.

The talent that is left is being driven out by bad administration. This may be a strategic attempt for districts to save money, but if talent is going out and no new talent is coming in, the infrastructure for student learning is not a good one. Teachers are like medical doctor's continually diagnosing and treating conditions of learning as well as providing treatment in many forms. They offer a variety of methods to heal a student's incapacity to learn. Interestingly, no one appears to question the amount of money a doctor makes or all the vacations and time off they take. I often hear comments such as, "doctors are highly educated and deserve it." Um yeah, well so are teachers.

Almost all teachers have a master degree and some even hold a doctorate. Besides, there are just as many kids messed up medically as there are educationally, so I would not be too quick to assess that the medical profession is doing a better job helping these young adults. Doctors don't seem to mind too much though because they are not being condemned and they are compensated very well for their lack of success.

Teachers, on the other hand are under constant scrutiny. I often wonder about the priorities of our nation; while schools are closing left and right, medical facilities are going up everywhere. The medical and pharmaceutical industry is booming and the educational system is falling apart. Maybe I am wrong, but this seems suspicious.

Dr. Krolczyk

Some things that I have seen negatively impacting the educational system include suspending kids, especially when the punishment doesn't fit the crime. In almost every circumstance, the student returns unmotivated to learn. As a matter of fact, they are discouraged to even come to school. I have also witnessed students that have mostly academic, rigorous classes, not allowed to leave for lunch. This lack of venue for their stress has led to an overall uneasy feeling making it difficult for them to continue to focus.

On the contrary, when I was in high school not only was I allowed to leave for lunch, but there even existed a courtyard that permitted an area for students to go and smoke. Now-a-days, if a student gets caught with an e-cigarette, it results in a 10 day suspension- which is ludicrous because this impacts, grades, learning, and possibly graduation.

Above all, loss of connection and intimacy between the student and the teacher and direct feedback is missing. Students knowing where to improve or where successes were made can be so incredibly vital to comprehension. The mere fact that students receive math tests back, in most cases with just a letter grade and no direct feedback should explain feelings of being overwhelmed and lost. These same students will be entering the workforce at some point and when the time comes for a supervisor to provide an evaluation their confusion will stem from not being conditioned to receiving feedback. Such conditioning will set them up for failure.

Additionally, breaking questions down into smaller sections so information is more manageable would immensely aid in the learning process. That is to say 62 questions compared to 12 is a big difference in memory recall. Further owing to the fact is the lack of life skills teens exhibit which has become quite concerning. For this reason, some may benefit from extra training in grammar, rhetoric, logic, and arithmetic (Cohen & Kisker, 2010, p. 183).

Another consideration affecting learning outcomes is virtual technologies. While useful in some respects, when students are being forced to go to school all day and then engage in virtual learning they encounter overload and simply shut down. Literary science speaks to how people have misguided views and investing in science and education can have implications in people's daily lives. This is because the educational process alone does not focus on the process of learning; it focuses on the outcome only which can be deceiving.

Timeline of Events that Shaped this Educational Crisis:

1. Parents wanted their kids to have "better" and "more" than they did.
2. Parents have exceeded this goal by giving their kids too much.
3. This overcompensation has caused kids to be lackadaisical.
4. Parents not wanting to admit they have given their children "too much" and made life "too easy for them" shift the blame to poor educational structures in the schools.
5. School officials not wanting to constantly battle with parents overtly aggressive behavior attempt to produce an image of learning without the engagement of learning *[lack of Student Capital].*

6. Rather than being appeased, parents' exhibit hostile behavior.
7. Parents then enter a depressive state due to overpowering guilt of transferring blame.
8. School systems are viewed as failing since students are not able to demonstrate a keen sense of knowledge.
9. The inability to perform is due to a culture exhibiting a false sense of wisdom.
10. Student's shortcomings leave them anxious.
11. The mental health industry capitalizes on human vulnerability.
12. Students continue to feel inferior until balance is restored.
13. Stability perpetuates from effort.
14. Continuous effort lends to accomplishment.
15. Having the right amount of vigor enhances the mind, body, and soul. *[Dr. Krolczyk's Model of Accomplishment]*

All of these measures have left students so overwhelmed some flat out refuse to come to school using anxiety/depression as the culprit. However, parents want accommodations so kids can still pass classes. Staying home and sending work back and forth to school does not help in the development of peer relations. According to Zunker (2016) peer relationships remain a challenge in that peer approval is of utmost importance. Socially responsible behavior becomes more relevant as individuals are faced with important decisions concerning the consequences of their choices.

The challenges students face at home and in school causes them a great deal of anxiety so their attendance starts to be affected and their mental well-being becomes questionable. USA Today reported it is hard to concentrate and do well in school if your brain has to constantly respond to stress (Toppo, 2015). The study conducted in USA Today that yielded such results also suggested students have more negative than positive feelings in relation to school, the top 3 being tired, stressed, and bored (Toppo, 2015). To put it briefly, the lack of support, accountability, parental involvement, lack of parenting skills and the parents' unwillingness to accept responsibility for their own actions can all contribute to a decrease in school attendance.

Evolving from adolescence to young adult is the most relevant period during the transitioning process (Zunker, 2016). At this age-level, students are less afraid of the consequences and repercussions of their actions as opposed to when they were younger. They depend less on their parents to assist with making educational decisions and feel that they are mature enough to do so on their own even if the decision is not wise.

However, these young adults are still young, which is why the sooner the parents become more involved, advocating for their child's educational needs while holding them responsible for their own actions and opening the lines of communication hence making them feel that their voice matters, the more confident and less stressed they will feel. These actions will assist with a decrease in anxiety/depression and an increase in school attendance (granted curriculum mandates change).

In order to build confidence and self-esteem, kids need to have an accurate perspective on life. How people view the world and how the world actually is can be disappointing. If a skewed sense of reality exists, a person may quickly blame society for their failures. This is much easier than facing the truth; however the easy route isn't always the best route. People may not realize all the talents and skills they have yet to unleash. Discovering what these talents are and developing these skills takes time, patience, and hard work. No one is going to walk up and hand someone their dream and that is the most important thing a person needs to understand. Dreams are created, not passed on.

A person will never aspire to reach their goals if they are continuously avoiding issues in hopes that someone else will resolve those issues. When a student has social anxiety, the worst thing a parent can do is email the school expecting schedule changes, teacher changes, or class hours to be moved around. The anxiety is the diagnosis; the managing of it is the treatment. Using it as a crutch will further delay freedom from the condition. Accommodations should be made within the structure of the issue, not around it.

Measures should be taken to help the student function within the constructs of daily life. Removing the student from situations that may be uncomfortable postpones therapeutic remedies from occurring. Coping mechanisms are difficult to put into place if avoidance is the prominent strategy. This is true of any ailment. No one else can believe in a person as much as they have the potential to believe in themselves. Only they know what they are capable of and proper guidance can help them discover this.

Students with mental health conditions need to be redirected to focus their energy on the best approach to face their situation. Excessive compassion from others at times can enable a person from doing this. Being equipped with techniques and skills so progress occurs is the best type of support that can be offered. When a student expresses they have anxiety about presenting in front of others, they should not be excused from having to do this.

They should understand that in order to be more comfortable giving presentations, they need to practice giving them. This can be done in front of a mirror, a friend, family members, or props. Videotaping has even proved effective as a means to view and determine strengths and weaknesses. Athletes use this technique all the time. People can even u-tube videos of dynamic presentations so they have a goal to aspire to.

There are so many things that can be done so a person can improve upon the act of presenting so in time they can be less anxious when having to speak publically. Kids are still developing and growing so they may not understand the benefit of learning how to communicate in front of peers. Just because they are unable to fathom the value in an activity does not mean they should be exempt from it. Discharging them from a skill that can be used to acquire success in life delays their independence. The reality is an individual can't expect to be excused from a situation and think their comfort level with this type of life activity is going to increase. Human behavior does not function that way.

It is not the condition of anxiety that governs actions; it is the regulation of their anxiety that determines outcomes. This is true in any case: speaking to the teacher, studying, homework, and test-taking, the best way to improve at something is to practice doing it. I had a student email me that she was anxious about taking tests, when I asked her to look at her behaviorism in preparation for exams, the underlying cause of her anxiousness was evident, she wasn't doing her own work and therefore did not know the material.

She also put little to no time in preparing for the exam. The method of managing her actions took place in the form of being heavily sedated and elongated meetings with the school. Rather, what she needed was a re-routing of behavior and to reflect upon her own conduct and make changes to achieve desired results. It also included reminding this young lady that a person gets out of something what they put into it.

There is something terribly wrong with our nation when mental health experts posit the increase in anxiety, stress, depression, and suicide can be attributed to the extreme pressure of academic rigor and subsequently national leaders roll out numerous initiatives to add more in-depth rigor to the curriculum, forcing students to be part of it by affiliating funding with these initiatives.

The government may as well hand students a gun and tell them to shoot themselves because killing our students is exactly what the nation is doing; physically and emotionally. Advanced classes are not for everyone, nor should these classes be. An all-inclusive approach is absurd. Students are individuals and should be treated as such thus allowing them the freedom of volition. Such freedom reduces anxiety and increases achievement.

No way in hell do I buy into the mentality that this nation knows what is best for every child, nor do I believe the focus is on students. If I had to take an educated guess, I would say the partnerships to increase academic programs for students of all races and income is politically driven for personal/company gain. I posit this because the strategies put into place to achieve these goals are hollow. Increasing student capital is about increasing student connections and helping them understand not only why something is important, but also how to achieve it. Kids need demonstrations of how to complete things so they can feel assured the direction they are taking is accurate and afforded the opportunity to ask questions if necessary.

Kids can learn just about anything in an environment where they are happy and safe. This type of environment exists by design, not default. I am disgusted that our nation is willing to risk student's mental health for financial capital. AP scores are down across the country, instead of evaluating why this is; a coalition exists to push more kids into these types of classes, as if this plan will miraculously solve the problem. Consequently, it creates an even bigger problem, the watering down of the AP curriculum and increased cheating. It also decreases opportunities for electives and skilled trade courses which students use as relief so they don't feel overwhelmed.

Kids see right through these blank strategies and do not feel efforts are sincere. I asked a student if he thought it was disrespectful to the teacher to cheat on his work and he replied, "She doesn't care about me, if she did, she wouldn't give me so much homework; I am so busy with homework I do not even have time to fill out college applications or apply for scholarships. If the teacher really appreciated my learning she would give me less homework and show me how to do it, then I wouldn't have to cheat."

The people making decisions on educational pursuits more than likely have not had these types of conversations with kids and therefore should not be considered experts in leading our future; they are contributors of mass destruction. Kids are overwhelmed and stressed, what part of that do national, state, and local leaders not get.

It has become a systematic error of lack of student capital. If schools want students to care about the subject matter then they need to show efforts of caring for the student. People mistake poverty for low performance but maybe the bigger issue is the shortage of care and concern. In my professional experience when compassion increases, so too does student performance. Care and concern is difficult to assess though a computer program, therefore it needs to come from the species of an actual living, breathing, physically present human being; not from a computer generated image of one. Online images or discussions simply do not have the same effect as in real time.

In the same fashion, schools need to be looked at as a place holder for what is going to happen later in life. It is a foundation for future endeavors. Solving new problems with old solutions doesn't work nor does engaging in complex challenges with simple solutions. The majority of complications a school experiences results from mismanagement or lack of proper investment in student capital.

Students that are able to move at a faster pace should be able to. Students that need more support should get it. For a competency based model to be effective the right resources need to be in place and professionals working with kids need to have accessibility to those resources. There should be shared decision making when determining supplies needed to acquire success. A paradigm shift needs to occur in how education is viewed because too many people are making poor choices that are severely impacting learning and that needs to stop if America is going to be great again.

Students are socially awkward, uninterested in school, circumventing schoolwork, have a skewed sense of careers, and are extremely immature. Forcing any of these components on them only hinders progress. Encouraging and showing students how to explore options, become involved, and take advantage of opportunities is the best way to attract and hold their attention.

Learning occurs on various levels, not just through books and lecture. Other methods of educating today's youth need to be implemented so all learning styles are addressed. This allows for a greater appreciation of knowledge being transferred and shared and with this foundation a student might discover their true passions.

Not to mention schools need to allow students early on the opportunity to fail so they can learn from that failure. Resources and tools are made available to students in high school and college and without a doubt; these resources should be simplistic and easily accessible. It is up to the student to utilize these resources to enhance their learning. If they don't know how, then they need to ask. Should they choose not to, well, that is their choice and they have to deal with the effect of it. However, as they mature and grow they may make different decisions based on the outcome of previous ones.

Lastly, kids need to know they are important. A lot of individuals have never had anyone tell them that. What kids value most is time spent with them. Everything I have learned about kids is from the connections I have with them. There is an association between thoughts, feelings, and comfort levels. A student may appear fine on the outside, but on the inside can be struggling immensely. If bonds are not formed such feelings will never be discovered. When a relationship exists, kids understand being held accountable is out of concern for their growth and development.

The same concept holds true for parenting. Childrearing needs to include kids being responsible and this liability starts with putting electronics away. Kids should not have head phones on scrolling social media sites while parents chauffer them around. They need to turn to their parents to aid in exploring the boundaries of life; not the internet. Parents need to enforce this so they are not in shock when a situation occurs. Kids need to become better at learning; parents need to become better at parenting. Tough love is harsh for a reason. Parents need to trust their judgment that they as the adult know what is best.

Future Endeavors

In the 1960's, there was a large need for remediation for students who were unprepared. This is significant because there appears to be a repeat of history with this current generation. Cohen and Kisker (2010), mention that in this time period the students coming out of high school where raised on early television and youth counter culture which glorified drugs and disrespect for authority. These same things are happening in today's society. These students are rude, lazy and rely on their parents to do everything for them. It really is déjà vu. Perhaps some of the distorted thinking rests upon being overly medicated. Society needs to move away from medication abuse.

Local and federal regimes need to realize the absurd burden being placed on students by not servicing them properly. At the same time, students need to seek out counselors or career experts to get a better grasp of coursework to pursue in high school that will better prepare them for college and/or a particular profession. Today's youths need to be cognizant of careers and credentials that matter to get a job that provides an honest income.

Entering a college undecided then through discussions, assessments, and awareness determining the best fit for a major might be the most appropriate route to take. Some students are even taking what has become known as a gap year. This is a year off after high school to travel, think, explore, and figure things out. Since senior year is not a magical journey with sunshine and unicorns, sometimes this gap year is exactly the break students need to rejuvenate their mind, body, and soul.

The looming question becomes how do we create a better nation without egregious failure? State legislators are grossly misinterpreting what it takes to educate today's youth thus causing an injustice to learning. Rather than look for ways to dispute this fact, educators need to focus on kids retaining valuable knowledge and encompassing skills that are employable.

Too much incorrect guidance has been given which has led to this disaster. Politicians have created a society of greed where people are more concerned with money than human growth. Such a lack of sensitivity has become more costly in the end trying to fix all the damage that has been done.

Change in educational practice put into effect sooner rather than later can prove cost effective. One of those changes needs to include students being afforded more opportunities for apprenticeships where they can explore and discover talents and interests. Other key factors of change include:

Less testing, more guiding
Less misguiding, more demonstrating
Less homework, more review
Less talking, more engaging
Less paperwork, more connectedness
Less technology, more personalization

Clearly the pattern is less equals more. By doing less, there is more time to implement the things that matter most, like professional learning communities with kids. This is where students have a shared sense of interest and work together to reach a common goal.

Student Capital

Since peers are powerful, students helping students has proven successful. An educator still needs to oversee the group in case information shared is inaccurate so as not to risk group think causing everyone in the cluster to have the information wrong, which doesn't help anyone.

It is also important to keep in mind accommodate does not mean "don't have to do" or is used to allow a student an "edge" over other students. It means alter the curriculum so the student can still acquire a sense of accomplishment and have an equal chance at learning. The simple formula below demonstrates expected outcome based on application.

Input = Output   Effort = Passing   No Effort = Failing

Furthermore, if simpler curriculum existed, teachers wouldn't have to keep accommodating assignments or tests. If less state mandated tests existed, teachers would have more time to focus on relationships with students. This is why having professionals that are experts in the field make decisions is a critical part of the learning process. Too much money, time, and energy is being spent on "fixing" the problem; when really all that needs to be done is a change in infrastructure.

Educators do not have time to foster relationships with kids because they are inundated with creating and filling out forms for accountability. There is only so much time in a day and if the majority of it is spent on bookkeeping, little is left for instructing.

Every time something "new" or "additional" is rolled out, teachers honestly do not know how they can ethically commit the time and attention to perform the task accurately. Any effort put into something new takes away from currently existing processes, therefore if a new strategy is supposed to be better, it should replace the old, not be added on as extra. The problem is, no one really knows if the new approach will be better, so they hold on to both, which only becomes confusing.

Teachers, whom are highly educated professionals, are more productive when they are able to work with kids without worrying about everything else. I have had students report they are afraid to ask their teacher a question because they know how stressed out their teacher is, this observation is not good at all for education.

Likewise, when parents are in a bad mood or stressed out kids are less likely to ask them anything. Eventually that mood dissipates and the child will then ask if the question entails something still important to them. I have seen messages in my kids' phones from them or another person saying, "I don't want to ask my parents, they are in a bad mood." What if that bad mood never goes away? What if it is present everyday all year long?

This is what students are observing in the schools and for fear that the frustration will then be transferred to them, they walk away never asking their question, never getting an answer, and never learning what they needed to know. Tell me one educator you know in the United States that is not exasperated.

The way things currently stand, education is being poisoned and as a result billions of government dollars will be spent on damage control. Why wait for that to happen when change can occur now. Grass roots efforts need to be put into place that incorporate schools, churches, and local businesses for a shared sense of community.

Theoretical strategies that cannot be correctly executed are meaningless. These types of dysfunctional endeavors from educational leaders need to cease. Start backing theory with resources from professionals in the field so people are not exhausting themselves running a race that never ends. Getting close enough to the finish line is not good enough if the finish line doesn't actually exist. When a person is led to believe one does, they keep running. Once they figure out it doesn't, they stop.

That is precisely what is occurring in education; teachers have stopped teaching in a way that helps students prepare for the finish line. They are helping students get to the race, and telling them to run, without students understanding which way, for how long, or why they are doing it. What could have been meaningful, no longer serves a purpose.

Again, teachers are so rushed all the time that connecting with students has been sacrificed. This is the epic American tragedy. Without the relationship much of what students do has no meaning. Bonding with one or two kids is not the same as thousands; which are how many students exists in most schools. Close affiliations with students is a strategy that works because students feel understood, important, and excited that someone believes in them. This type of acceptance arouses and motivates a person to want to do more because when people feel good they are inspired. Social media is similar to the race that never ends; people are left unfulfilled.

My daughter recently posted a picture of her and her little brother on Halloween; she received 215 likes. When she showed me this, my first thought was that I don't think I know that many people, let alone have that many friends, secondly why are so many likes important. She indicated because people she doesn't know that well will see how good she is with her brother and they will think she is a nice person. She is allowing people she barely knows to control her actions. I explained to her that if she was a good person people would take note regardless of what picture she posts that offers the impression of being a good person.

Teens have become so neurotic about their status in the virtual world they are literally driving themselves crazy with worry and concern about what others think. The reason they care so much what people think virtually is because people do not know how to express it verbally. Therefore they rely on others they barely know to instill confidence in their actions by clicking a button that offers approval; which is a very slippery slope.

Youths of today have become so insecure they think someone giving them a dirty look in the hall constitutes bullying. They want everyone and their mother to make that person stop because they simply cannot handle it. Because people looking at other people cannot be stopped; hypersensitivity exists and skews one's thinking. My daughter is a very pleasant young lady and should not concern herself with what twitter thinks. Now she has experienced an unparalleled sense of reality and has expectations that are flawed. She will more than likely keep obsessing with posts until she surpasses 215.

Can you imagine the nightmare of this being a teenager's greatest concern? For some students, that is the only relationship they have so their ideation of success is impracticable. If connections were available in the school, someone could work with students and help them identify this. Students are so confused they are just shutting down.

I equate this to telling my kids we are going to go on a fabulous vacation, and then we are going to finish our basement, and put a pool in. My kids start jumping up and down and are very excited. They ask me "when" is this is all going to happen, and I respond, "Oh, we don't have any resources to make this happen; your dad and I just thought it would be nice to plan." Then I tell the kids, "Hey, let's be creative and use the resources we have." I am almost certain one of my kids would point out, "but mom, we do not have the correct resources." I guarantee if I were to respond, "That' ok, let's just do the best we can," they will have a forlorn look on their face and walk away.

At that point, I lost their interest, excitement, and engagement by promising them something I am able to deliver. It doesn't matter how many times I draw designs for the basement, look at pool stores or research vacations, until the money is available to do these things the kids are not going to buy into those plans. Now, if I were to tell them to use the resources we have to build a birdhouse there is good chance this would get done because that goal is realistic.

That is indeed what is happening with educating today's youths across the globe. Initially success is falsely elevated moreover when a student moves on and perhaps doesn't experience success quite as easily, they are unable to handle this disappointment. Such displeasure can be devastating thus causing them not to want to do anything.

They certainly can still achieve success; they just would have to put forth effort. Somehow students internalize this blow feeling demoralized, worthless, defeated, and hurt. For some students it may take years to recover and other students may never recuperate causing a downward spiraling effect.

I recently spoke to a director of human resources that mentioned he wished more graduates were, "work ready." I asked him to describe what he meant by work ready and he replied, "They want to work."

What kind of nation have we become where we have young healthy people that have no desire to work? Young adults have been given so much during their existence that they are blindsided to the true value and meaning of life. In fact, many youths have become so comfortable with marijuana use they are unable to pass a drug test for employment; which stresses them out so they get a prescription for anxiety, collect SSI, and stay home all day.

Everyone else is blamed for their misery while they sit home wallowing in self-pity and continue to smoke marijuana. Self-motivation, self-improvement, self-confidence, self-esteem all contain the root word self. Until a person realizes that, their life will not change.

I used to think integrity was the most important skill a person could possess, not anymore. I truly believe genuineness is the best skill a person can have. A person can give the impression they act with integrity, when indeed they do not. However, if a person is genuine, there are no false impressions. When a person has sincere intentions, the pureness of actions radiates.

Take ER for example, there exists a separate section for pediatrics, yet multiple patients are geriatrics and there is no section specific for them. Why not? Elderly people's needs are different than that of the average population and if hospitals are going to express genuine concern for these residents than a geriatric ward should be instituted. What makes sense often is not what organizations do.

Parents assert they want their kids and grandkids to have it better than they did. Better, however, does not have to be a bigger home and fancier car, better should be a nation built on pride and respect. Work ethic is not something a person is born with, it is taught, instilled, nurtured, and redirected. People believe they deserve luxurious things they didn't work for and this has become a big problem.

Look at some celebrities for example; many of them after they make their fortune go broke because they were overspending on items they didn't need to impress people that didn't even care about them. Too often society falls into this trap.

People need to use ethical courage so they will know what to say and do in difficult situations and cope with the pressures of modern times. Even learning how to meditate can make people feel more at peace. Training the mind to think good thoughts rather than bad ones has been proven in theory to help acquire happiness.

Kids need individual post high school planning. Part of the reason they don't do anything is because they don't know what to do. Many students have asked, "I applied to college, now what?" Kids actually need personal guidance all throughout high school. When selecting classes, adolescents take courses that are easy, not necessarily what is best for them. Why? Because they are teenagers and that is what youngsters do?

Everyone gives in to them instead of informing them of what is best. Somewhere, at some point, they fall apart. Some students have phenomenal GPA's, but no testing skills. There are other students that graduated with A's in English, but get to college and can't write a paper. Adults are appalled when this happens, and are unwilling to consider the possibility that the student never did anything to earn that "A", and by not doing anything, they didn't learn anything.

To exasperate matters, kids continually worry about what others think not realizing another's opinion of them is irrelevant to who they are. Since teacher class sizes and counselor caseloads are disproportionate to job duties and responsibilities, no one is available to discuss pertinent matters with students. Everyone ends up arguing with everyone else. In retrospect:

*Teacher unions are fighting with teachers
*Police are fighting with citizens
*Aggression, anxiety, depression, and homicide are all on the rise
*Curriculum is watered down
*Learning is superficial
*Self-esteem is at a national low
*Kids are uninterested in learning
*Parents are too busy to parent
*Teachers are disconnected with students

I have a vision where aggregations of mankind demonstrate probity in preserving all humanity. As human beings we are becoming desensitized to terrorist attacks, mass shootings, suicides, dysfunctional educational systems, financial greed and disrespectful teens. This is very, very, concerning and must change for future generations to prosper. The best years of your life are when you chose to control your destiny, no one else, just you.

REFERENCES

American Psychiatric Association (2013). *Diagnostic and statistical manual of mental disorders, fifth edition (DSM-5)*. Arlington, VA: American Psychiatric Association.

American School Counselor Association (2016). *Why secondary school counselors?* Retrieved from https://www.schoolcounselor.org/school-counselors-members/careers-roles/why-secondary-school-counselors

Center for Disease Control (2016). *Mental health; Anxiety.* Retrieved from http://www.cdc.gov/MentalHealth/basics/mental-illness/anxiety.htm

Chapman University (2016). *Are you a first generation college student*? Retrieved from https://www.chapman.edu/students/academic-resources/first-generation/

Cohen, A., Kisker, C., (2010). The shaping of American higher education. San Fransico, CA; Jossey-Bass.

Curtis, A. C. (2015). Defining adolescence. *Journal of Adolescent and Family Health, 7*(2), 1-39. Retrieved http://scholar.utc.edu/cgi/viewcontentarticle=1035& context=jafh

Gordon, J. (2014). *The carpenter: A story about the greatest success strategies of all*. Hobokon, NJ: John Wiley & Sons, Inc.

Hosny, M. and Fatima, S. (2014). Attitude of students towards cheating and plagiarism: University case study. *Journal of Applied Sciences,* 14: 748-757. Retrieved from http://scialert.net/fulltext/?doi=jas.2014.748.757

Kleinman, P. (2012). *Psych 101: A crash course in the science of the mind.* Avon, MA:Adams Media.

Mayo Clinic (2016). *Serotonin Syndrome.* Retrieved from http://www.mayoclinic.org/diseases-c conditions/serotonin-syndrome/basics/symptoms/

Mathews, J. (2006). *The weak case against homework.* Retrieved from the Washington Post.com. Website: http://www.washingtonpost.com/wp-dyn/content/article/2006/11/21/AR2006112100633

Michigan Department of Education (MDE) (2016). *Mental health.* Retrieved from http://www.michigan.gov/mde/0,4615,7-140-74638-199286--,00.html

Moore, G., Slate, J., Edmonson, S., Combs, J., Bustamante, R., Onwuegbuzie, A. (2010). High school students and their lack of preparedness for college: A statewide study. *Education and Urban Society. 42*(7); 817-838. Retrieved from http://journals.sagepub.com/doi/abs/10.1177/00131

Morrison, J. (2014). *DSM-5 made easy.* New York, NY: The Guilford Press.

Pope, J. (2006). *Admissions board faces grade inflation.* Retrieved from The Associated Press. Website: http://www.washingtonpost.com/wpdyn/content/article/2006/11/18/AR2006111800473_pf.html

Seligman L., & Reichenberg L., (2014). *Theories of counseling and psychotherapy: Systems, strategies, and Skills.* Upper Sadle River, NJ: Pearson Education, Inc.

State News (2016). *MSU counseling services to undergo massive restructuring.* Retrieved from http://statenews.com/article/2016/11/msu-counseling-to-be-restructured

Toppo, G. (2015). *Our high school kids: Tired, stressed, and bored.* Retrieved from USA Today. Website: https://www.usatoday.com/story/news/nation/2015/10/23/survey-students-tired-stressed-bored/74412782/

Wolfe,D. & Mash, E. (2006). *Behavioral and emotional disorders in adolescents: Nature, assessment, and treatment.* New York, NY: The Guilford Press

Zunker, V. (2016). *Career counseling: A holistic approach*. Boston, MA: Cengage Learning

APPENDIX A

Terms

AP
Advanced Placement

CR
Credit

EL
English Learner

GRANTS
Money given that does not need to be paid back

MI=MDD
Mass instruction equals mass destruction + mass deception

MoA
Model of Accomplishment; finding balance between *mind, body, and soul*

NEEDING-ACTING GAP
What a person or company needs is not what the person or company does.

NC- No Credit
When a student would have passed a class, but credit is taken away due to poor attendance

STUDENT CAPITAL
Increasing student connections to help youths understand the purpose of doing things and demonstrating how to do it so they can reach a level of success that helps them feel accomplished.

UNIQUE IDENTIFICATION CODE (UIC)
This is usually a number assigned to each individual student and a way to identify him/her.

***WHY* AND HOW GAP**
People understand *why* they should do things; they just don't know *how* to do it.

APPENDIX B

Career Resources

2017's Most in Demand Jobs

https://www.betterteam.com/job-descriptions

**This website offers job descriptions of various careers, potential salary, projected job growth, and states where this career is most popular. In the top right hand corner of each job field is "view job spec" if you click on this, you will be given more details about the description of the career, qualifications, and skills needed to succeed in that profession.

Occupational Outlook Handbook

https://www.bls.gov/ooh/

**This website offers a statistical analysis of pay, education level, and prospective growth for many careers. It also details a description of the job, working conditions, and training.

O'NET Online

https://www.onetonline.org/

**This source offers tasks, skills, technology, knowledge, abilities, and under credentials-training-colleges with degree programs in any given field in any given state.

My Next Move

https://www.mynextmove.org/

**This software program permits a search for careers by keywords, industry, or interest profiler (take an interest inventory test).

Bright Outlook

https://www.mynextmove.org/find/bright

**The site shows careers growing rapidly, with lots of openings, and occupations that are new or emerging.

Registered Apprenticeship

https://www.mynextmove.org/find/apprenticeship

**This offers a detailed list of apprentice programs registered U.S. Department of Labor.

AP Credit Policy Search

https://apstudent.collegeboard.org/creditandplacement/search-credit-policies

**Follow the link below. In the search box- type in any college, in any state, to see what AP score is needed that institution to grant college credit.

Michigan Transfer Agreement

https://www.macrao.org/Publications/MTA.asp

This is a fabulous site that allows for a person to check what classes at a community college would transfer to university.

1. Under student services (left hand side) find *Transfer Equivalency*
2. Public and private colleges will display
3. Select the college you would like to explore; follow directions on that page on how to match up courses.

Federal Student Aid: FAFSA

https://fafsa.ed.gov/

This is the official site that needs to be used when filling out the FAFSA. It also offers tips and tools to use to determine family contribution.

National Association of Student Financial Aid Administrators: NASFAA

https://www.nasfaa.org/students_parents_counselors

This is an excellent, easy to maneuver, resource on types of financial aid, factors in determination, and insight on mistakes to avoid.

About the Author

Dr. Krolczyk is a high school guidance counselor, college professor and professional counselor in private practice. She has over twenty years of experience within the school and college setting. She is an expert at counseling adolescences helping them to prepare for college and careers while building optimistic self-esteem in a nation with much uncertainty. She serves as a consultant for career technical and adult education and is extremely passionate about helping students find their inner strength so they can develop a level of balance for a greater sense of wellbeing. She has been asked by state organizations to reshape educational policy and has given multiple presentations addressing the concerns and needs of today's youths. Her focus is on educational reform and creating a better infrastructure for the schools and mental health systems. She holds degrees from: Walsh College, Wayne State University, University of Detroit Mercy and Central Michigan University. She resides in Michigan with her husband and their four children.

Made in the USA
Monee, IL
06 January 2022

88041748R10256